D1274840

10 BOOKS THAT SCREWED UP THE WORLD

10 BOOKS THAT SCREWED UP THE WORLD

And 5 Others That Didn't Help

BENJAMIN WIKER, Ph.D.

Author of *Moral Darwinism: How We Became Hedonists*

Since 1947
REGNERY PUBLISHING, INC.
An Eagle Publishing Company • Washington, DC

Cataloging-in-Publication data on file with the Library of Congress

ISBN 978-1-59698-055-6

Published in the United States by
Regnery Publishing, Inc.
One Massachusetts Avenue, NW
Washington, DC 20001
www.regnery.com

Manufactured in the United States of America
10 9 8 7 6 5 4 3 2 1

Books are available in quantity for promotional or premium use. Write to Director of Special Sales, Regnery Publishing, Inc., One Massachusetts Avenue NW, Washington, DC 20001, for information on discounts and terms or call (202) 216-0600.

Every good faith effort has been made in this work to credit sources and comply with the fairness doctrine on quotation and use of research material. If any copyrighted material has been inadvertently used in this work without proper credit being given in one manner or another, please notify the publisher in writing so that future printings of this work may be corrected accordingly.

*To my wife of twenty-five years, without whom
the world would be much poorer, and with whom
my life has been infinitely richer.*

Contents

Ideas Have Consequences

"THERE IS NOTHING SO ABSURD," QUIPPED THE ANCIENT ROMAN philosopher-statesman Cicero, "that it can't be said by a philosopher." Unfortunately, philosophers' absurdities aren't limited to classroom sophistry and eccentric speculations. They make their way into print and are thereby released upon the public. They can be, and have been, as dangerous and harmful as deadly diseases. And as with deadly diseases, people can pick up deadly ideas without even noticing. These ideas float, largely undetected, in the intellectual air we breathe.

If we take a good, hard, sober look at the awful effects of such deadly ideas we can come to only one conclusion: there are books that really have screwed up the world, books that we would have been better off without.

This should not come as a shock, except to those who don't believe that ideas have consequences. Thomas Carlyle, the eminent Scottish essayist and sometime philosopher, was once scolded at a dinner party for endlessly chattering about books: "Ideas, Mr. Carlyle, ideas, nothing but ideas!" To which he replied, "There once was a man called Rousseau who wrote a book containing nothing but ideas. The second edition was bound in the skins of those who laughed at the first." Carlyle was right. Jean-Jacques Rousseau wrote a book that inspired the ruthlessness of the French Revolution (and even more destructive things after that).

Common sense and a little logic tell us that if ideas have consequences, then it follows that bad ideas have bad consequences. And even more obvious, if bad ideas are written down in books, they are far more durable, infecting generation after generation and increasing the world's wretchedness.

I submit, then, that the world would be a demonstrably better place today if the books we're about to discuss had never been written. It was possible half a century ago (and even twenty years ago, among the academic elite) to maintain that Marxism was a positive force in history. But since the protective cover has blown off the Soviet Union—and China's has at least been torn—no one can look at the tens of millions of rotting corpses revealed and conclude anything other than this: if the *Communist Manifesto* had never been written, a great deal of misery would have been avoided. The same is true of Hitler's *Mein Kampf* and the other books on the list, even when the carnage is sometimes of a more subtle and different sort.

What then? Shall we have a book burning? Indeed not! Such a course of action is indefensible, if only for environmental reasons. As I learned long ago, the best cure—the only cure, once the really harmful books have multiplied like viruses through endless editions—is to *read* them. Know them forward and backward. Seize each one by its malignant heart and expose it to the light of day. That is just what I propose to do in the following pages.

Part I
Preliminary Screw-Ups

CHAPTER ONE

The Prince
(1513)

"Hence it is necessary to a prince, if he wants to maintain himself, to learn to be able not to be good. . . ."
Niccolò Machiavelli (1469–1527)

YOU'VE PROBABLY HEARD THE TERM *MACHIAVELLIAN* AND ARE AWARE of its unsavory connotations. In the thesaurus, *Machiavellian* stands with such ignoble adjectives as *double-tongued, two-faced, false, hypocritical, cunning, scheming, wily, dishonest,* and *treacherous.* Barely a century after his death, Niccolò Machiavelli gained infamy in Shakespeare's *Richard III* as the "murdrous Machiavel." Almost five hundred years after he wrote his most famous work, *The Prince,* his name still smacks of calculated ruthlessness and cool brutality.

Despite recent attempts to portray Machiavelli as merely a sincere and harmless teacher of prudent statesmanship, I shall take the old-fashioned approach and treat him as one of the most profound teachers of evil the world has ever known. His great classic *The Prince* is a monument of wicked counsel, meant for rulers who had shed all moral and religious scruples and were therefore daring enough to believe that evil—deep, dark, and almost unthinkable evil—is often more effective than good. That is really the power and the poison of *The Prince*: in it, Machiavelli makes thinkable the darkly unthinkable. When the mind is coaxed into receiving unholy thoughts, unholy deeds soon follow.

Niccolò Machiavelli was born in Florence, Italy, on May 3, 1469, the son of Bernardo di Niccolò di Buoninsegna and his wife, Bartolemea de' Nelli. It is fair to say that young Machiavelli was born into wicked times. Italy was not a single nation then, but a rat's nest of intrigue, corruption, and conflict among the five main warring regions: Florence, Venice, Milan, Naples, and the Papal States.

Machiavelli witnessed the greatest hypocrisy in religion, including cardinals and popes who were nothing more than political wolves in shepherds' clothing. He also knew firsthand the cold cruelty of kings and princes. Suspected of treason, Machiavelli was thrown into jail. To elicit his "confession," he was subjected to a punishment called the *strappado*. His wrists were bound together behind his back and attached to a rope hanging from a ceiling pulley. He was hauled up in the air, dangling painfully from his arms, and suddenly dropped back to the ground, thereby pulling his arms out of their sockets. This delightful process of interrogation was repeated several times.

Machiavelli knew evil. But then, so did many others, in many other times and places. There is no shortage of wickedness in the world, and no shortage of witnesses to it. What makes Machiavelli different is that he looked evil in the face and smiled. That friendly smile and a wink is *The Prince*.

The Prince is a shocking book—artfully shocking. Machiavelli meant to start a revolution in his readers' souls, and his only weapons of revolt were his words. He stated boldly what others had dared only to whisper, and then whispered what others had not dared even to think.

Let's look at Chapter Eighteen for a taste. Should a prince keep faith, honor his promises, work above board, be honest, that kind of thing? Well, Machiavelli muses, "everyone understands" that it is "laudable . . . for a prince to keep faith, and to live with honesty."[1] Everyone praises the honest ruler. Everyone understands that honesty is the best policy. Everyone knows the countless examples in the Bible of honest kings being blessed and dishonest kings cursed, and ancient literature is filled with tributes to virtuous sovereigns.

But is what everyone praises truly wise? Are all good rulers successful rulers? Even more important, are all successful rulers good? Or does goodness, for a ruler, merely mean being successful, so that whatever leads to success—no matter what everyone may say—must be good by definition?

Well, says Machiavelli, let's see what actually happens in the real world. We see "by experience in our times that the princes who have done great things are those who have taken little account of faith." Keeping your word is foolish if it brings you harm. Now, "if all men were good, this teaching would not be good; but because they are wicked and do not observe faith with you, you also do not have to observe it with them."

But keeping one's word is not the only thing that should be cast aside for convenience. The whole idea of being good, Machiavelli assumes, is rather naïve. A successful prince must concentrate not on being good, but on appearing to be good. As we all know, appearances can be deceiving, and for a prince deception is a good thing, an art to be perfected. A prince must therefore be "a great pretender and dissembler."

And so, one might ask, should a ruler be merciful, faithful, humane, honest, and religious? Not at all! It is "not necessary for a prince to have all the above-mentioned qualities, but it is indeed necessary to appear to have them. Nay, I dare say this, that by having them and always observing them, they are harmful; and by appearing to have them they are useful." So it is much better, more wise, "to appear merciful, faithful, humane, honest, and religious," but if you need to be cruel, faithless, inhumane, dishonest, and sacrilegious, well, then, necessity is the mother of invention, and you should invent devious ways to do whatever evil is necessary while appearing to be good.

Let me offer two examples of Machiavelli's advice in action, the first taken from *The Prince*, and the other from our own day. A more wicked man than Cesare Borgia—whom Machiavelli knew personally—could hardly be imagined. He had been named a cardinal in the Catholic Church, but resigned so he could pursue political glory (and did so in the most ruthless way). Borgia was a man without conscience. He had no anxiety whatsoever about inflicting great cruelties to secure and maintain power. Of course, this gave him a bad reputation with his conquered subjects, creating the kind of bitterness that soon leads to rebellion. In Chapter Seven Machiavelli sets before his reader an interesting practical lesson on Borgia's method of dealing with this problem.

One of the areas Borgia snatched up was Romagna, which Machiavelli notes was a "province . . . quite full of robberies, quarrels, and every other kind of insolence." Of course, Borgia wanted "to reduce it to peace and obedience," because it is hard to rule the unruly. But if he brought them into line himself, the people would hate him, and hatred breeds rebellion.

What did Borgia do? He sent in a henchman, Remirro de Orco, "a cruel and ready man, to whom he gave the fullest power." Remirro did the dirty work, but of course this got him dirty. The people hated Remirro for his attempts to crush their rebellious and lawless spirit and make them obedient subjects. But as Remirro was obviously working as Borgia's lieutenant, Borgia would be hated too.

But Borgia was an inventive man. He knew that he needed to fool the people into believing that "if any cruelty had been committed, this had not come from him but from the harsh nature of his minister." And so, Borgia had Remirro "placed one morning in the piazza at Cesena [cut] in two pieces, with a piece of wood and a bloody knife beside him. The ferocity of this spectacle left the people at once satisfied and stupefied."

Satisfied and stupefied. The angry people of Romagna were happy to see the agent of Borgia's cruelty suddenly appear one sunny morning hewn in half in the town square. Borgia himself had satisfied their desire for revenge! But at the same time they were numbed into obedience by a completely unexpected spectacle of ingenious brutality.

The reader's imagination gropes after an image of the horror. A man sawed in half. Lengthwise or crosswise? A bloody knife. Simply lying beside the body? Thrust into the block of wood? Could a mere knife hack a man in two? And why a block of wood? A butcher's block?

One thing is certain: Machiavelli does not blame Borgia for his ingenious cruelty, but praises him. He very cleverly appeared to be humane by hiding inhumanity, to be merciful by concealing mercilessness. "I would not know how to reproach him," Machiavelli says of Borgia's lifelong career of similar dastardly actions. "On the contrary, it seems to me he should be put forward, as I have done, to be imitated by all those who have risen to empire through fortune."

One does not always need to be as viciously picturesque as Borgia to follow Machiavelli's advice. As anyone who watches our own political scene well knows, we quite often witness the less bloody (but no less well calculated) spectacle of an underling to a president or congressman immolating himself publicly to take the heat off his boss. Behind the elaborately staged appearances, the underling— like poor Remirro, who was merely carrying out the chief's orders— is being sacrificed to satisfy and stupefy the electorate.

This brings us to our second example of Machiavellianism in action. "A prince should thus take care," notes Machiavelli, returning to his list of virtues, "that nothing escape his mouth that is not full of the above-mentioned five qualities" so that "he should appear all mercy, all faith, all honesty, all humanity, all religion. And nothing is more necessary to appear to have than this last quality." It is most important that rulers—and even more so, would-be rulers—appear to be religious. "Everyone sees how you appear," but "few touch what you are," and appearing to be religious assures those who see you that, because you appear to believe in God, you can be trusted to have all the other virtues. In politics, some things never change.

But duplicity isn't the only patrimony of Machiavelli's *The Prince*. The damage is much deeper than that. The kind of advice Machiavelli offers in *The Prince* is only possible for someone to give (and to take) who has no fear of hell, who has discarded the notion of the human soul living on after death as a foolish fiction, who believes that since there is no God then we are free to be wicked if it serves our purposes. That is not to say that Machiavelli ever advises being evil merely for its own sake. He does something far more destructive: evil is offered under the excusing pretext that it is beneficial. Machiavelli convinces the reader that great evils, unspeakable crimes, foul deeds are not only excusable but praiseworthy if they are done in the service of some good. Since this advice occurs in the context of atheism, then there are no limits on the kind of evil one can do if he thinks he is somehow benefiting humanity. It should not surprise us that *The Prince* was a favorite book of the atheist V. I. Lenin for whom the glorious end of communism justified any brutality of means.

Since this will remain an important connection in most of the subsequent books we cover, we must dwell on the deep connections between atheism and the kind of ruthless advice Machiavelli gives. It is a fundamental principle of Christianity—the religion that defined the culture into which Machiavelli was born, and the religion he rejected—that it is never permissible to do evil in the service of good. You can't lie about your credentials to get elected to office. You can't kill an innocent baby to advance your career. You can't start a war to boost the economy or your approval ratings. You can't resort to cannibalism to solve the hunger problem. You can't commit adultery to get a job promotion.

The source of this prohibition is obviously the fact that some actions are intrinsically evil. No matter the circumstances or the alleged or even actual benefits, some acts cannot be committed. Unfortunately, this is not the way we generally think today. When you suggest to someone that there are some intrinsically evil actions—so foul, so unholy, that even to think of doing them leaves a black mark on the soul—the usual response is a smirk, followed by a wildly contrived example that is supposed to force you into choosing some horribly evil deed to avoid even more horrible consequences. "What if a terrorist gives you a choice: either shoot and skin your grandmother or we'll blow up New York." The hidden assumption of the smirker is that, of course, the moral thing to do is save New York by shooting and skinning your grandmother, and that goes to show that there are no moral absolutes.

Of course, smirkers are rarely logical. If there really are no intrinsically evil actions, then it is quite fine to have New York blown up in order to save your grandmother. But the real point, for our purposes, is that the smirker is using precisely the mode of reasoning that Machiavelli uses in *The Prince.* Machiavelli is the original ends-justify-the-means philosopher. No act is so evil that some necessity or benefit cannot mitigate it.

But how is this all linked to atheism? Again, we must use the religion that historically defines the beliefs Machiavelli rejected. For the Christian, no earthly necessity or benefit can be weighed against eternity. Committing an intrinsically evil act immediately separates us from the eternal good of heaven, whatever the benefit that might accrue to us in the here and now. No good we experience now can possibly outweigh having to suffer eternally in hell. Furthermore, as God is all-powerful, then no seeming necessity or benefit of an evil action in this life can really be necessary or beneficial to anyone from the perspective of eternity. To believe otherwise is only a temptation; in fact, *the* temptation.

As we shall see in subsequent chapters, yielding to the temptation to do evil in the service of good will be the source of unprecedented carnage in the twentieth century, so horrifying that to those who lived through it, it seemed hell had come to earth (even though it was largely perpetrated by people who had discarded the notion of hell). The lesson learned—or that should have been learned—by such epic destruction is this: once we allow ourselves to do evil so that some perceived good may follow, we allow ever greater evils for the sake of ever more questionable goods, until we consent to the greatest evils for the sake of mere trifles.

Remove God, and soon there is no limit on evil at all, and no good is too trivial an excuse. Consider a report from the British newspaper *The Observer* three years ago: in the Ukraine, suffering so long under the atheist Soviet foot, pregnant women were being paid about $180 for their fetuses, which the abortion clinics turned around and sold for about $9,000. Why? The tissue was being used for beauty treatments. Pregnant women were and still are being paid to kill their babies so aging Russian women can rejuvenate their skin with fetal cosmetics.

But to return to Machiavelli, our point is this: to embrace the notion that it is not only permissible but also laudable to do evil so that good might come, one must reject God, the soul, and the afterlife. That is just what Machiavelli did, and that is the ultimate effect of his counsel.

Here it might be objected that Machiavelli appeared to be religious in his writings, casting out pious phrases here and there, and speaking with a certain respect (however strained and peculiar) about things religious. So, it is argued, because he appears to be religious, then we must give him the benefit of the doubt.

It is difficult for me to deal with this all too common objection because it shows a frightening woodenness to the obvious (let alone to the subtle) in Machiavelli. Did he not just tell us how important it is to appear to be religious? Who informed us of the necessity, if one is to be a great prince, of being a great pretender and dissembler? Who contrives to be a greater prince—the temporal ruler of a piece of land, or the philosopher who seeks to inform all future princes, to found an entirely new philosophy?

And so we repeat: Machiavelli could not give advice to princes that would mean abandoning any notion of God, the immortal soul, and the afterlife if he himself had not already abandoned all three. That is why he can call evil good, and good evil.

This is seen clearly in the famous Chapter Fifteen. Machiavelli tells the reader quite matter-of-factly that he is departing from the way all others have spoken about good and evil. He will deal with the real world, with how people act in real republics and principalities. While "many have imagined republics and principalities that have never been seen or known to exist in truth," we realists shouldn't take our sights from mere fantasy. We cannot guide our lives by what is good (or at least what is called good), Machiavelli warns us; we must guide our lives by what is effective. "For a man who wants to make a profession of good in all regards must come to ruin among so many who are not good. Hence it is necessary to a prince, if he wants to maintain himself, to learn to be able not to be good, and to use this and not use it according to necessity."

In reality versus the imagination, Machiavelli chooses *realpolitik*. But where are these imaginary republics he so strenuously rejects? One would be in Plato's *Republic*, in which Socrates argues that human beings must strive, above all, to be good. Another would be in Cicero's *On the Republic*, which argues much the same thing. But Machiavelli's most important rejection is that of the Christian notion of heaven. He makes this rejection quite clear elsewhere (in his *Discourses on Livy*) when he argues that the prospect of heaven ruins our attempts to make this life—our only real life—better.

Christianity, Machiavelli contends, focuses our energies on an imaginary kingdom in the sky and thereby turns us away from making the real world a peaceful, comfortable, even quite pleasurable home. Moreover, Christianity ties our hands by moral rules—backed up by the imaginary stick and carrot of hell and heaven—so that we cannot do the necessary dirty work. Machiavelli thereby initiates the great conflict between modern secularism and Christianity that largely defines the next five hundred years of Western history, and in this respect, *The Prince* shows its mark in all the rest of the books we will examine.

CHAPTER TWO

Discourse on Method (1637)

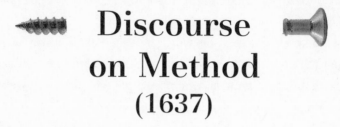

> *"I reject as absolutely false everything in which I could imagine the least doubt...."*
>
> René Descartes (1596–1650)

HOW GRATEFUL WOULD YOU BE IF YOU CAME TO ME COMPLAINING of a headache and I chopped off your head? Certainly, I fixed the problem—and permanently so!—but at a rather higher cost than you'd hoped for.

René Descartes' *Discourse on Method* has had a similar effect on the Western mind. Descartes' little book has done damage to us precisely by seeming to do good, like a bull who kindly offers to straighten up the china shop. Descartes attacked skepticism, but only by denying reality. He confirmed the idea of the immaterial soul against the pronouncements of the crass materialists of the day, but only by recreating us as insubstantial ghosts trapped in clattering machines. He proved God's existence, but only by making it depend on our thinking Him into existence. By his good intentions—if indeed they really were good—he fathered every flavor of self-congratulatory solipsism, led us to believe we are no different from robots, and made religion a creation of our own ego. Thanks a lot, René.

If we take Descartes at his word, he was seeking a way around the snarling skeptics of his day. Skepticism is a kind of intellectual disease that generally arises among people who are both well fed and well read. No one who is truly hungry worries about whether it is possible to know whether the steaming hamburger in front of him is real. In fact, ordinary people working under quite natural conditions are not bothered by skepticism at all. Imagine a farmer wandering around lost in his own thoughts, vexed by the question of whether we can really know what a cow is. He is too immersed in reality to question it. The cow needs to be milked and there's no time for udder confusion.

One could wish that Descartes had a cow staring at him impatiently. I say this not because it is a bad idea to refute skeptics—that is one very good service philosophers can do for farmers—but because it is a very bad idea to do it with a cure that's worse than the disease. Good intentions can make for bad medicine.

Descartes begins the *Discourse on Method* with a joke. "Good sense," he tells us, "is the most evenly distributed commodity in the world, for each of us considers himself to be so well endowed therewith that even those who are the most difficult to please in all other matters are not wont to desire more of it than they have."[1]

In short, everyone is satisfied with his own opinions, and thinks anyone who doesn't agree a fool. This would be quite harmless if human beings merely disagreed about the best flavor of ice cream or other matters of mere taste. But each has his or her own opinion about the deepest and greatest questions as well. Whether God exists, and if He does, what He demands of us. What actions are good or evil, moral or immoral, noble or base, fair or foul. What political parties should be voted in, and what should be done by the winning party.

If you doubt the bite of Descartes' little joke, then look around during an election year. We have two political parties, each of which can barely suppress disagreements among its own members long enough to oppose the other. Abortion, prayer in school, homosexual marriage, federal subsidies, welfare, war. During an election year, the well-worn adage "Talk about anything but religion, morality, and politics" is cast aside so we can talk about nothing but. The resulting acrimonious cacophony reminds us of the wisdom of having presidential elections only every four years.

The fact that we all disagree about so many things makes us skeptical that we can know anything at all. If we could really know the truth about something, then it would seem that people couldn't disagree about it. Maybe it's all a matter of mere opinion after all. Maybe the skeptics are right.

This skepticism is what Descartes meant to cure. He offered a method as medicine, pretending with false modesty that he wasn't really saying that everyone should follow his method, but merely describing what method had worked for him.

This false modesty hid a gargantuan pride. Descartes desired nothing less than that everyone should follow his method, and his wish has been all too handsomely fulfilled. He is known—and rightfully and woefully so—as the father of modern philosophy. If you think that doesn't pertain to you, the great Frenchman Alexis de Tocqueville said after his visit to America in the first half of the nineteenth century that "America is...one of the countries where the precepts of Descartes are least studied and are best applied."[2] I leave it to discerning readers of Tocqueville's *Democracy in America* to determine whether that was a compliment. But his point was that Descartes' philosophical method had somehow seeped into our souls and become second nature.

What, then, is Descartes' method? Simply put, doubt everything. In order to conquer skepticism, Descartes proposed that we be skeptical about everything to see if there is anything left we can't be skeptical about. "I thought it necessary," he tells us in Part IV of the *Discourse*, "that I reject as absolutely false everything in which I could imagine the least doubt, so as to see whether, after this process, anything in my set of beliefs remains that is entirely indubitable."

Before we jump on Descartes' bandwagon, we should ask the most obvious question: isn't this a rather doubtful process? What if we took it the other way around? Should we accept as absolutely true everything in which we can discern the least grain of certainty? Why would this be any less rational than rejecting everything in which we can imagine the least bit of doubt? It is possible to imagine the tree I am about to walk into is not solid at all, but actually made of mist. After caroming off it, I might have other ideas.

But such a method would seem to be madness, and it soon gets even madder. A good recipe for insanity is this: that *I* reject as absolutely false everything in which I could imagine the least doubt. If we let our imaginations run wild, we could doubt even the solidity of the ground we stand on or the fact that we have a nose.

Even if such a method doesn't lead to insanity, it certainly leads to narcissism, the morbid condition of believing that I sit in god-like judgment of everything else but nothing stands in judgment of me. We suspect that Descartes' method clothes itself in the most abject humility as a way to exert the most naked pride. It assumes the posture of a quivering ant to presume the imposture of a towering god.

But before we get carried away in criticizing his method, we ought to follow it out. What does Descartes say must be doubted? First, all wisdom from the past, whether it be found in books or in tradition. The past has nothing to teach Descartes. Why? Because there is disagreement, and disagreement must mean an absence of wisdom.

There is, for example, not one philosophy in one book handed to us from the past, Descartes points out, but many contradictory philosophies in a multitude of conflicting books. It isn't a matter of I.Q. Even among "the most excellent minds who have ever lived...there is nothing about which there is not some dispute" in philosophy, "and thus nothing that is not doubtful" (Part I). Where there is disagreement, there is doubt, and where there is doubt, throw it out.

Nor is tradition a valid guide, Descartes informs us. There is not one tradition among all people, but many incompatible traditions among wildly dissimilar people. Indeed, there seems to be no underlying common human nature at all, for "the very same man with his very own mind, having been brought up from infancy among the French or the Germans becomes different from what he would be had he always lived among the Chinese or among cannibals" (Part II).

The more we look at the great thinkers, so Descartes tells us, the more confusion we find. The more we examine the traditions of our own country as compared to those of other countries, the more everything seems to be relative. All is shifting sand.

But even more must be doubted. Our senses sometimes err. We see things that aren't really there. We hear noises and misidentify what they are. What to do? Descartes "decided to suppose that nothing was exactly as our senses would have us imagine."

If that weren't enough, we must doubt even reason. As we find ourselves making errors in reasoning, even in mathematics, Descartes decided to reject "as false all the reasonings that I had previously taken for demonstrations."

Finally, as we think we are awake when we are dreaming, and experience things as real in dreams, "I resolved to pretend that everything that had ever entered my mind was no more true than the illusions of my dreams."

And what was left after this scorched-earth approach? According to Descartes:

> ...during the time I wanted thus to think that everything was false, it was necessary that I, who thought thus, be something. And noticing that this truth—*I think, therefore I am*—was so firm and so certain that the most extravagant suppositions of the skeptics were unable to shake it, I judge that I could accept it without scruple as the first principle of the philosophy I was seeking (Part IV).

There we have it, one of the most famous phrases in the history of philosophy: *I think, therefore I am.* Or, in its more famous form, *cogito ergo sum.* The *Discourse,* however, was originally written in French, and so we have "*je pense, donc je suis,*" where the "I" (French, *je*) has the same egotistical emphasis as the English version.

Sounds convincing, doesn't it? If it does, congratulations! You've just walked into a trap that has ensnared the Western mind for four centuries. It is a trap from which there is no escape because Descartes has presented it as itself an escape—but it is an escape from a trap that doesn't exist.

Skepticism is a problem in our minds. It is a deadly trap only if we retreat into our minds to escape it. That is, if we let our doubt turn into doubt about reality. The place to run to escape skepticism is not our own minds, where the spider of solipsism waits to devour us, but straight into a tree to remind ourselves that, whatever our fancy to the contrary, the real world outside our minds has been factually solid all along. The proper and natural treatment for those inclined to think themselves into a corner is not to go into a corner and think but to run out into the fields to grasp and be grasped by reality.

But we must dig deeper into Descartes' fundamental error. On a lesser level, it is simply ridiculous to single out thinking as the act by which I know I am existing. One could just as easily use hearing, smelling, or coughing (except, perhaps, that they don't sound nearly as good in Latin: *audio ergo sum; odoror ergo sum; tussio ergo sum*). I am not denying that thinking is more fundamentally human than hearing, smelling, or coughing, but only calling attention to the point that Descartes' argument is not somehow essentially tied to thinking. It is only this: that while I am doing X (whatever X is), I cannot doubt my existence because I have to exist to do X.

On a deeper level, the snappy dictum "I think, therefore I am" contains one of the most pernicious confusions possible, so destructive that we might very well call it the first sin. We catch the error if we lapse for a moment into common sense and say, "Well, René, isn't it really the other way around? In order to think, I first have to exist, and I go right on existing even when I am not thinking. And anyway, didn't the world get along just fine before I was ever around to think about anything? So we should say, 'I am, therefore I can think,' rather than, 'I think, therefore I am.'"

The common sense point is this: reality exists before our thinking, so that our thinking depends on reality, and this in two ways. First, our thinking depends on the reality of our own existence. If we don't exist, we can't think. Second, our thinking correctly depends on our properly conforming our minds to what really exists. Scientific theories are judged true or false, better or worse, insofar as they actually correspond to the way things are in the real world. Against Descartes, we assert common sense against nonsense:

the first principle of philosophy is reality (or being), not "I think." Reality trumps.

If we ignore this first principle, and take Descartes' instead, our imaginations untethered to reality can only run wild, as he himself giddily demonstrates. "I could pretend that I had no body and that there was no world nor any place where I was, but...I could not pretend...that I did not exist." And what does he conclude? "From this I knew that I was a substance the whole essence or nature of which was merely to think, and which, in order to exist, needed no place and depended on no material thing."

Obviously this absurdity was not uttered near lunchtime. In any case, reality had the last say over Descartes' imagination: he died of a cold. I know how hard it is to think when I have a cold. Perhaps he fell victim to his own dictum and ceased for a few fateful minutes to think! *Non cogito, non ergo sum.*

But this little instructive frivolity aside, the next step in Descartes' argument is yet more baneful. What assures him that his maxim is true, he tells us, is that "I see very clearly that, in order to think, one must exist," and so "I judged that I could take as a general rule that the things we conceive very clearly and very distinctly are all true."

It looks as if Descartes has anticipated our objection here, for he now admits that "in order to think, one must exist." We'll see in a bit if he's really conceded this point to common sense. But for now we must note the egregious error he's slipped in.

Would it really be a good idea to accept as "a general rule that the things we conceive very clearly and very distinctly are all true"? I remember, about ten years ago, very clearly and very distinctly seeing a tell-tale mess of white paint all over my garbage can in the alley behind our house, and I very clearly and distinctly noticed that the peculiar lady next door (who regularly slipped things into our garbage can because she was too cheap to pay for her own trash service) was painting her kitchen white because I very clearly and distinctly *saw* her carrying around a whitened paintbrush as she very clearly and distinctly *told* me she was painting her kitchen white, and I *imagined* myself very clearly and distinctly grabbing her by her tattered sweater and dragging her back to clean up the very clear and distinct mess all over the garbage can and surrounding pavement. Fortunately, while I was out back staring at the white paint and imagining even more vicious revenge, upon closer inspection I noticed that the white glop was white wallboard plaster, not white paint. The mess was actually made by the man redoing our bathroom. The lady next door was entirely innocent (of that, at least).

But this isn't just a moral lesson. Again, it regularly occurs in the history of science. We'll cite one interesting instance. A number of prominent scientists, beginning in 1877 with Italian astronomer Giovanni Schiaparelli, were convinced that they saw through their telescopes an intricate system of canals on Mars. These canals were all very geometrical and hence obviously carried water for the great Martian civilization. The certainty of intelligent life on Mars was trumpeted (with the aid of businessman and amateur astronomer Percival Lowell). Books were published. Major newspapers declared the evident certainty to the astounded (and gullible) public. Helping to whip the public into a frenzy was alien enthusiast H. G. Wells, whose *War of the Worlds* seared into people's minds the dire fate that awaited Earth once the Martians stopped boating around their canals and launched their inevitable attack.

By 1930, this certainty was exploded by another astronomer, E. M. Antoniadi, who pointed out that the "canals" weren't canals; they weren't nice geometrically drawn lines of precision traced on the surface of Mars, but just fuzzy shapes.

The lesson is simple enough. Schiaparelli, Lowell, Wells, and a host of other scientists and popularizers wanted to see life on Mars. The alien enthusiasts just wanted to see what was fuzzy as straight and geometrical because they wanted Mars to be populated with aliens. It is often our desire to have something be true that makes us clearly and distinctly see the false as true, the imagined as real. This is as true in the history of science as it is in our everyday life. In either case, reality is the appropriate test of our everyday beliefs and scientific theories.

In contrast to this salutary realism, Descartes' method of doubting everything but his own thought, has, for us poor moderns, made subjectivism the criterion of truth. But methodical egoism (the Latin for "I" is *ego*) isn't the only bad thing Descartes sent down the river to us. The very way he defined the "I" has also befouled the historical stream. Recall Descartes' strange conclusion: as he could imagine that he had no body and that there was no material world, therefore he "was a substance the whole essence or nature of which was merely to think, and which, in order to exist, needed no place and depended on no material thing."

A ghastly conclusion, or rather a ghostly one, for by it Descartes imagined that we were pure spirits trapped in alien bodies (or more accurately, as we soon find out, alien machines). As Descartes reveals in Part V of the *Discourse on Method*, he is a raving mechanist who believed that all nature was nothing more than machinery. Animals and plants are no more alive (or dead) than hydraulic pumps, toasters, or alarm clocks. Even more, our human bodies are merely self-running machines.

Hence Descartes is also known as the father of modern dualism. Dualism is the belief that human beings aren't one thing—an intimate and essential union of soul and body—but two entirely different and independent entities, a ghostly soul banging around in a ghastly machine.

If Descartes is the father of modern dualism, what does dualism itself beget? A walking philosophical bipolar disorder, a creature who is not at home in creation, a creature who dwells in dual extremes, either as wholly a ghost or entirely a robot. One day he feels that he is a god, a purely spiritual being, capable of completely mastering and manipulating all nature (including his own body) as he would any machine, and the next day believes that he is a purely material being, a helpless machine entirely mastered by the mechanics of nature.

This brings us to Descartes' final error, his absolutely awful proof of the existence of God (in Part IV). We recall that Descartes puts as the first principle of his philosophy "I think, therefore I am." He then asserts that God must exist because he (Descartes, not God) can think of a being more perfect than himself. Therefore, he concludes, "this idea was placed in me by a nature truly more perfect than I was...and...this nature was God." To make matters worse, Descartes then claims that it must be the case that his ideas, "insofar as they are clear and distinct, cannot fail to be true" because they too come from God. Therefore, God exists, because Descartes can imagine Him, and all Descartes' clear and distinct ideas are absolutely true, because God put them there!

I pray that readers can see the foolishness of this reasoning. I can think of a man or woman who is more perfect than any I've ever met. Does that mean either of them necessarily exists? I can think of a superior alien race existing on a much nicer planet than Earth. Does either exist? Our thinking of anything is not proof that it exists, let alone proof that whatever seems to me to be "clear and distinct" is given a divine stamp of authority, as if God put it there.

Descartes' approach to religion is not only false, but creates the characteristically modern belief that God is whatever we "very clearly and very distinctly" imagine Him to be. And that means we fashion God after our own hearts, rather than our hearts and religion after God. This doesn't just lead to bad belief, but even worse, to bad non-belief. If God is whatever we very clearly and distinctly imagine Him to be, then if we can very clearly and distinctly imagine Him not to be, He isn't. *To be or not to be*, that becomes the modern quandary about God. But the horns of this dilemma are largely chimerical; that is, they are the horns of a mythical beast created by Descartes' imagination. His beastly reasoning has led us to reject God on the grounds that our thinking about Him is fuzzy, and to accept the most ridiculous utopian fantasies about humanity because we can imagine them quite clearly and distinctly. Marxism is only the most obvious instance of the pernicious working out of Descartes' ideas, but, as we shall see, not the only one.

What are the principal errors we can thank the father of modern philosophy for? First, subjectivism, which is really a thinly disguised form of egoism. We have become Cartesian insofar as we declare that there is no wisdom in the past, and that whatever seems to be certain to us now must be true. Rather than leading us to greater wisdom and independence of thought, we become far more likely to affirm thoughtlessly our own unexamined opinions. Since these unexamined opinions are generally obtained from the frivolous ideas bandied about in the contemporary marketplace, we end up in the very situation Descartes satirized at the beginning of the *Discourse*, where everyone is satisfied with his own opinion simply because (so he believes) it is his own and so it must be true.

This has led to a second evil: the confusion of true wisdom about God with whatever one happens to think about God. This, of course, is the ultimate egoism, since in defining God by our own thoughts, we define everything else accordingly. A third evil then follows from the first two, that reality is defined by what we think it to be. Descartes wanted to imagine he was some kind of disembodied ghost and that his own body and everything in nature were merely machines. The problem with this dualism is that it soon became a monism: the ghost disappeared and we were left only with the machine. Thus, even human life came to be reduced to mere mechanism—something that could be taken apart and rebuilt according to our own desires. The second and third evil then gave birth to a fourth. Since God was caused by our thinking Him, then He must only be a thought and not a reality, a mere subjective projection of our own ego. Since He is not real, then He does not stand against whatever we desire to do with the machine of nature, especially the machinery of the human body. We are free to manipulate it at will, and remake human nature according to our own plans, so that we can really say, in a far deeper way than Descartes, "I think, therefore I am." Rather than taking ourselves to be made in the image of God, with all the moral limitations that entails, we believe that we are self-creators with no limit but our own ever-increasing power.

CHAPTER THREE

Leviathan
(1651)

"Every man has a right to every thing. . . ."
Thomas Hobbes (1588–1679)

ACCORDING TO THOMAS HOBBES, THERE IS, BY NATURE, NO GOOD and evil, right and wrong, just and unjust. Left to ourselves, independent of society and in our natural condition, we are creatures entirely without conscience, ruled solely by pleasure and pain, ravenous in our desires and ruthless in their pursuit. If that redefinition of human nature weren't bad enough, Hobbes added the insidious notion that human rights are simply equivalent to human desires (however sordid), so that whatever we happen to desire, we have a right to by nature. Thus Hobbes is the father of the all too familiar belief that we have a right to whatever we want—however morally degraded, vile, or trivial it may be—and further, that it is the government's job to protect such rights.

We have become so Hobbesian that it is difficult for us to see his beliefs as shocking, and what Hobbes really said is so shocking that it is doubly difficult for us to believe he could ever have put the words to paper. That is the importance of wading through the arguments of his monumental work, *Leviathan*. It allows us to see the foul headwaters of the stream in which we swim. How, then, to begin?

Imagine waking up one morning and feeling quite suddenly that someone had removed all the burdens of conscience, all your subterranean naggings and hesitations. You are now entirely relieved of any inner contradiction to each and every desire. The walls of opposition you used to associate with something called "conscience" are simply gone. As you soon realize, once these barriers vanished, your thoughts and desires wandered freely over previously unknown and uncharted territory.

Completely without conscience. No recognition of right or wrong, good or evil, light or dark. The distinctions have ceased to have any real meaning—or they have taken on a new meaning. Good simply means getting whatever you want, and evil is anything that might stand in your way of getting it. You are now Hobbes's natural man, man as he truly is by nature.

Or are you? Have you gone far enough? Have you really peeled away all the accretions of conscience and arrived at Hobbes's natural man? My suspicion is that if you are "conservative," you are thinking only of removing the walls of conscience over which you are likely to climb, and that if you are "liberal," you are thinking only of removing the walls of conscience built by conservatives. But we are talking no walls at all. Raping for fun, killing for pleasure, torturing for amusement, cannibalizing your near relations, and yes, torching the rain forests just to witness the splendid spectacle of destruction and to hear all the animals, especially the endangered ones, scream in terror and pain.

"Whatsoever is the object of any man's appetite or desire, that is... [what] he for his part calleth *good*: and the object of his hate and aversion, *evil*;... for these words of good and evil... are ever used with relation to the person that useth them; there being nothing simply and absolutely so; nor any common rule of good and evil to be taken from the nature of the objects themselves."[1] Get it? No sin. "The desires, and other passions of man, are in themselves no sin. No more are the actions, that proceed from those passions."[2] So declared Thomas Hobbes a bit over three and a half centuries ago.

If no one is around to make us feel guilty, and we can for a moment banish any thought of divine retribution, this all might seem inviting, liberating, exhilarating. Until you realize—as your neighbor carries off your wife and your newspaper boy smashes your windows (aided by the sheriff, who then proceeds to strafe your house with bullets, trying to write his name on your aluminum siding)—that everyone else woke up just as you did, entirely relieved of all their burdens of conscience. You recognize that, rather than being blissfully free to fulfill your previously forbidden desires while everyone else behaves, you are plunged into "a war, as is of every man, against every man," in which there is "continual fear and danger of violent death," so that your life is very likely to be "solitary, poor, nasty, brutish, and short."[3]

It then hits you like a brick. Or rather, as a brick just flew through the window and hit you, you immediately apprehend that "to this war of every man, against every man, this also is consequent; that nothing can be unjust. The notions of right and wrong, justice and injustice have there no place. Where there is no common power, there is no law: where no law, no injustice. Force, and fraud, are in war the two cardinal virtues."[4]

Stanching the flow of blood with your pillowcase, you look in the direction the brick came from and find that your other neighbor, who's already fired up his outdoor grill, is offering a strangely insistent invitation that you dine with him this morning. And now, all at once, you come full in the face to the "fundamental law of nature." "Because the condition of man...is a condition of war of every one against every one; in which case every one is governed by his own reason," for anyone and everyone, "there is nothing he can make use of, that may not be a help unto him, in preserving his life against his enemies." Therefore, "it followeth, that in such a condition, every man has a right to every thing; even to one another's body."[5]

Even to one another's body! That's why the neighbor on one side carried off your wife when she stepped out the front door looking for the morning paper. That's why the neighbor on the other wants you for a barbeque. Welcome to the "state of nature."

This was, of course, an imaginary exercise. But is it an imaginary state? In one sense, it seems not, because it captures all too accurately the kind of barbarism that surfaces in the midst of war. But is human nature at its worst the best place to begin to study humanity? Hobbes thought so, and his great innovation (or one of them) was to assume that human beings at their worst give us a horrid but accurate glimpse of what they really are once the veneer of civilization is ripped away. Having witnessed the savagery of men during war—he wrote *Leviathan* just after the Thirty Years' War (1618–1648) and during the English civil wars that occurred in the mid-seventeenth century—Hobbes concluded that war was natural and peace unnatural, that butchery and barbarism are innate while charity and civility are entirely artificial, that the real garden of nature is a killing field and the bucolic Garden of Eden a pitiful pipe dream.

We must dwell upon this last point. It is characteristic of the authors we're examining that, as they are nearly all atheists, they passionately desired to replace the biblical account of human origins with one of their own contriving. In fact, in many respects all of modernity is an attempt to replace the biblical account of Eden with an entirely new story (just as it is an attempt to replace a heavenly kingdom with an earthly utopia). For our purposes, it doesn't matter whether you think the Edenic account is a fable, because the really important thing is to see that one story about human nature and human origins is being replaced by another. Hobbes's state of nature is a new revelation, a counter-Genesis account meant to reveal what we really were at the very dawn of humanity and hence what, deep down, we truly are now. But it is entirely a fiction.

Please drink in these words, swirl them around in your soul, meditate upon them: Hobbes's state of nature is entirely a fiction. A myth. A fable. A tall tale. An utterly imaginary state. Neither Hobbes nor anyone else living in the seventeenth century could have had a clue about what human origins were really like. Archaeology wasn't even in its infancy. But even more obvious, if human beings had been like Hobbesian men and women at the dawn of humanity, the nightfall of humanity would quickly have descended through self-destruction. How could families ever have begun and grown into tribes if men were little more than bloodthirsty killers and wandering rapists, and women became cannibals soon after they became mothers or simply bashed in the heads of their offspring because they found them inconvenient?

Sane critics of Hobbes pointed out almost immediately upon *Leviathan*'s printing that his state of nature was a complete fiction. So if it was seen as a complete fiction then, and we can see it as one now, why go on about it? Because it is an enduring fiction. It is becoming, more and more, the myth by which we live. *Leviathan* has become our Bible, and Hobbes's state of nature our Edenic myth.

Think not? See if you can spot the most fatuously fictional aspect of his reasoning: "Because the condition of man…is a condition of war of every one against every one; in which case every one is governed by his own reason," for anyone and everyone, "there is nothing he can make use of, that may not be a help unto him, in preserving his life against his enemies." Therefore, "it followeth, that in such a condition, every man has a right to every thing; even to one another's body."

Which is the most egregiously fantastical fiction? Is it that our natural condition is one of war? Is it that, in our natural state, everyone is governed by his own reason (meaning, for Hobbes, that each person acts like a cunning, ruthless Machiavellian)? Is it the assertion that primitive human beings naturally and easily resort to cannibalism when they run out of coconuts?

No, it is the groundless claim that "every man has a right to every thing." It is hard for us to spot the fatuity because "rights" talk has largely overtaken our public and political discourse, rudely shoving moral speech out of the way. Hobbes meant to shove it out of the way, and to do it he concocted out of the thinnest air his entirely fictional notion of rights. According to this toxic fantasy, rights are simply equivalent to desires, so that "I have a right to do X" is merely another way of saying "I have a desire to do X."

Once we've seen the invention of such rights claims, we can recognize that in our Hobbesian world the statement "I have a right to pornography" is merely a restatement of "I have a desire to view pornography." "Mary has a right to marry Susan" really only means "Mary has a desire to marry Susan." This can take more complicated and roundabout forms. "I have a right to control my own body" is a veiled way of stating "I desire an abortion." "I have a right to privacy" might really mean "I really want to do stuff that would nauseate my great-grandmother." "I have a right to free speech," which sounds noble and defensible as a right, could really be a more compact and disingenuous way to say "I have a desire to shock Christians and delight the artsy intelligentsia of New York by dropping a crucifix in urine."

Hobbes established these fictional rights not by argument but by mere definition, i.e., by bald declaration (and few people were as bald as Hobbes, as his portraits attest). "The right of nature . . . is the liberty each man hath, to use his own power, as he will himself, for the preservation of his own nature; that is to say, of his own life; and consequently, of doing any thing, which in his own judgment, and reason, he shall conceive to be the aptest means thereunto."[6] Of course, this leads to all-out war, as each person pursues anything and everything he desires.

Hobbes's reasoning (hidden and open) leading up to this declaration is as follows:

1. There is no God.
2. Therefore there is no good or evil.
3. Human beings are merely physical creatures who have no other meaning or goal in life but to feel physical pleasure and avoid physical pain.
4. The notions of "good" or "evil" arise because human beings call what brings them physical pleasure "good" and what gives them physical pain "evil."
5. Since there is no God, and no good or evil by nature, there is no limit to what anyone can do to get what he desires, and no limit to what he can do to avoid physical pain.
6. Therefore each of us is free (has "liberty") to do anything he wants to preserve his own life. This is the "right of nature."

7. As life is defined merely as the endless pursuit of pleasure and avoidance of pain, then the preservation of life includes the endless pursuit of pleasure and the prevention of any possible obstacle by any possible means.

8. And that means utter chaos, or a "state of war."

But while Hobbes drove us into a state of war, he didn't leave us there. He offered a way out, an escape that has screwed up our entire understanding of society because it became the foundation of modern liberal political theory and practice. Hobbes imagined that human beings are naturally antisocial individuals who enter society only because they are trying to escape the dangers of the state of nature. This escapist fiction is so enduring that it has become endearing, so we need to examine it with care and critical distance.

The dangers that make our natural, pre-social state a "state of war" are brought about, argues Hobbes, precisely because each individual believes he has a right to everything and anything he desires. These pre-social individuals would remain in the state of nature if they could, because (so they think) it is always better to get whatever you want whenever you want it.

But because everyone else is bursting with rights/desires, there is complete chaos in which anyone could be killed and eaten. So these rights-frenzied creatures reluctantly enter a society by making a kind of agreement that—here comes the escape clause—each "man be willing, when others are too . . . to lay down this right to all things" and "be contented with so much liberty against other men, as he would allow other men against himself."[7]

This all gives us a rather strange view of society as something alien to our nature. In the Hobbesian view, society is neither good nor natural. It is at best a necessary evil, an entirely artificial contract between isolated and essentially hostile individuals in order to avoid a "poor, nasty, brutish, and short" life in the state of nature. That in turn produces an entirely negative view of justice. "I won't do X to you if you won't do X to me." We are not bound by love. We have no feelings of natural duty to our family or our neighbor, and no noble affection for the people and place of our birth. Rather, we are bound by mutual distrust and animosity.

It is not surprising that Hobbes's negative and ignoble view of human nature and human society yields a negative and ignoble view of justice. It is doubly unsurprising that his view consequently produces a notion of government drained of all but the lowest motives. A Hobbesian society is one in which each person considers himself first and foremost as an individual brimming with rights/desires but with no fundamental responsibility to anyone else. For the Hobbesian individual, then, it is the entire job of government to protect and maximize the expression of these individual rights/desires while simultaneously minimizing conflict with other rights/desires–bearing individuals. In short, the one and only task of government is merely to reproduce a happier version of the Hobbesian state of nature, where there is a maximum of liberty to pursue one's personal desires but without the nasty, violent death part.

Hobbesian justice is therefore understood as a kind of inversion of the golden rule: don't do unto others, so they won't do unto you. Or, if we could put it in a longer, positive form that is more familiar: let others do what they want (as long as whatever they do is not directly hurting you), so that you may do whatever you want (as long as you are not directly hurting others).

The underlying assumption of this view of justice, we recall, is the Hobbesian belief that there is by nature no good and evil. That the words *good* and *evil* mean only "That feels good to me" and "Ouch! I don't like that!" respectively. The result is that morality becomes merely a private thing, a thing of personal taste, so that

"I think abortion is wrong" or "I think pornography is wrong" are no more or less moral statements than "I don't like chocolate ice cream" or "I can't abide chartreuse." This complete moral relativism is behind the great Hobbesian protest of our time: "No one has a right to tell me what to do." Note the emphasis on *right*, as in Hobbesian rights/desires, and not on *right* as in right and wrong.

The interesting thing about Hobbesianism—if you tend to be interested in the macabre—is that it becomes a kind of self-fulfilling prophecy. That is, although his chaotic state of nature was originally an unseemly fiction, if a society acts according to Hobbes's notion of rights, then it becomes, increasingly, a fractious, rights-demanding, passion-driven collection of self-willed individuals hell-bent on getting whatever they desire no matter the cost, and all the while claiming they have a right to what leads to their own and society's self-destruction.

Perhaps that is why you might have a feeling of déjà vu when you read Hobbes's *Leviathan.*

CHAPTER FOUR

Discourse on the Origin and Foundations of Inequality among Men (1755)

"Savages are not evil precisely because they do not know what it is to be good. . . ."

Jean-Jacques Rousseau (1712–1778)

JEAN-JACQUES ROUSSEAU HAS DONE SO MUCH DAMAGE IN SO MANY books that it is hard to single out one element, let alone one book, for censure. But for our purposes, we can in good conscience zero in on his *Discourse on the Origin and Foundations of Inequality among Men*, a cornucopia of profound confusion whose rotting fruit has seeded several generations of subsequent errors.

The *Discourse* was signed "Jean-Jacques Rousseau, Citizen of Geneva," denoting where he had been born more than forty years before. Rousseau's life did not begin well. Sadly, his mother died within a few days of his birth, leaving him to be raised by his aunt and his unstable father, a wandering watchmaker who had spent only two years of his married life with his wife before she died. Fleeing the law, he then abandoned the young Rousseau when the boy was ten. A boy without a family, Rousseau moved from relatives to apprenticeships, socially clumsy and sickly, growing into manhood with little or no guidance as he meandered about Europe from job to job (engraver, copyist, lackey, tutor, secretary, land register, assistant to an ambassador), from patron to patron, and from mistress to mistress.

Rousseau loved romance, disliked labor, and more than anything despised even the smallest hint of authority that might make him beholden to some master, no matter how mild or reasonable. That accounts for his difficulty in holding any position for very long. It was also largely because of this loathing of authority that he was for the most part self-taught, reading intensely and indiscriminately. As a result, Rousseau combined brilliant and original insights with embarrassing and harmful blunders.

One illustration to demonstrate the point. Rousseau adored music and fancied himself to be quite gifted. But because he was self-taught and perhaps had mild dyslexia, he had great trouble reading standard musical notation. He decided to invent his own system of notation, thinking that his ingenious improvement would make him rich and famous. After he presented it to the prestigious Académie des Sciences, the teachers there pointed out to him that, although the new notation of the melody was quite creative, it could not represent harmony. A rather obvious drawback, but relatively harmless. However, Rousseau made the same kind of mistake when attempting to work out ingenious improvements in political philosophy. As these affected real people, they were quite harmful indeed.

At the age of thirty-eight Rousseau finally achieved fame, winning an essay competition in 1750 offered by the Academy of Dijon. The Academy proposed the question: "Has the restoration of the sciences and arts tended to purify morals?" Rousseau's answer, given in his *Discourse on the Sciences and Arts*: "No. The more civilized we become, the more corrupt we become." He claimed that the advance of the sciences and arts took people away from their original, natural purity and happiness, making them both softer and more elaborately vicious. The same is true, he argued, even for the art of government. While government and laws provide for our safety, they take away our "original liberty," so that we become "happy slaves" with "delicate and refined taste," who have a "softness of character and urbanity of customs" that give "the semblance of all the virtues without the possession of any."[1] We would all be infinitely more virtuous, asserted Rousseau, if we were noble and rustic Romans, or even better, noble but entirely uncultured savages. "The good man is an athlete who likes to compete in the nude."[2] So spoke Rousseau in his *First Discourse*.

Rousseau's *Second Discourse*—properly titled *Discourse on the Origin and Foundations of Inequality among Men*—was an expansion of this theme. It was written in response to yet another question posed by the Academy of Dijon, this time in 1754: "What is the origin of inequality among men, and is it authorized by natural law?" This time Rousseau didn't win the prize (his essay generously exceeded the required length), but it did win lasting fame when Rousseau had it published the following year.

I called the *Second Discourse* a cornucopia of profound confusion. The word "cornucopia" should awaken us to the richness and overflowing abundance of Rousseau's work. Even as we demonstrate its confusion, we should not underestimate its profundity. Simple-minded errors rarely engender great historical results, and Rousseau's was no simple mind. One finds in him, for good or ill, the seeds of Romanticism and folk-nationalism, the French Revolution and totalitarianism, Marx and Nietzsche, Freud and Darwin, modern anthropology and Margaret Mead, the sexual revolution and the dissolution of the family—all marked with what is characteristically Rousseau: genius and blunder. Let's peruse both.

Rousseau used the Academy's question about inequality as a pretext to push his reasoning in the *First Discourse* to the extreme, in an effort to find "natural man," man as he is in the "state of nature." "The philosophers who have examined the foundations of society have all felt the necessity of going back to the state of nature, but none of them has reached it,"[3] declared Rousseau, obviously having Thomas Hobbes's efforts in mind (as well as those of John Locke).

But Rousseau's differences with Hobbes shouldn't blind us to the great similarities. To begin with, as with Hobbes, we find ourselves in a powerful fiction, an imaginary time sketched by the author that allegedly provides such great insight into what human nature really is. Rousseau seems to call attention to his fiction when he warns the reader that he is "setting all the facts aside" and that what he has to say "must not be taken for historical truths, but only for hypothetical and conditional reasonings."[4] Yet one can easily suspect Rousseau of Machiavellian duplicity: he knew full well that what he had to say smacked of heresy, and he had no wish to tangle with church authorities. But Rousseau's little deceit aside, we must stress the point that, given the state of historical and anthropological researches at the time, his picture of primitive or natural man can only have been painted from his own imagination.

We stress this because it proves to be a pattern for many modern intellectuals. Their imaginations run away with them, and they run away with their imaginations. They fashion a utopia in the distance, either in the mists of the distant past or the sunlit slopes of the distant future. By the power of their words, they drive otherwise sane and healthy men and women to waste their own lives and the lives of countless others, sometimes to the ruination of their countries.

What, then, did Rousseau imagine? If we might be a bit glib, whereas Hobbes's men in the state of nature were gorillas—nasty, brutish, and curiously short—Rousseau's primitive men were suave, peaceful, innocent, carefree, and cheerfully libidinous bonobos. Rousseau therefore gave us a new Adam, a carefree, make-love-not-war ancestral archetype who became the societal ideal of the "free love" movements.

According to Rousseau, natural men "in the primitive state" had "neither houses, nor huts, nor property of any kind." Indeed, they were little more than animals. They had no language; they were creatures of the senses, not of reason. As in Hobbes's vision, these original human beings were naturally solitary. Neither love nor the family was natural. "Males and females united fortuitously, depending on encounter, occasion, and desire," and "they left each other with the same ease."[5]

Rousseau goes so far in his imaginative destruction of love and the family that he denies even the love of mother and child. "The mother nursed her children at first for her own need; then, habit having endeared them to her, she nourished them afterward for their need. As soon as they had the strength to seek their food, they did not delay in leaving the mother herself; and as there was practically no other way to find one another again than not to lose sight of each other [in the jungle or forest], they were soon at a point of not even recognizing one another."[6]

And the father? Well, as it turns out, the concepts of fatherhood and moral duty—even the concept of "love"—are artificial contrivances that arise only after men have declined from the morality-free primitive state. How so? Primitive men and women acted only on sexual impulse. "Everyone peaceably waits for the impulsion of nature, yields to it without choice with more pleasure than frenzy; and the need satisfied, all desire is extinguished." In other words, one-night stands didn't even last one night. Happily, primitive people weren't picky. Because man is so primitive, he has no idea of beauty: "any woman is good for him."[7] As for his string of offspring, given that he's off into the trees once his "need" is "satisfied," "he did not recognize his children"[8] even if he happened to stumble upon them later on.

There you have it: Rousseau's paradise, his new and improved Adam and Eve. Sex entirely devoid of all the unpleasant duties and entanglements of love! A mere "blind inclination, devoid of any sentiment of the heart," that produces "only a purely animal act," satisfying a passing brute desire. And when the desire is quenched, "the two sexes no longer recognized each other, and even the child no longer meant anything to his mother as soon as he could do without her."[9] Every cad's paradise! Paternity without strings! No pestiferous pangs of conscience!

There were no twinges of conscience for natural man, Rousseau assured the reader, because "the moral element of love is an artificial sentiment born of the usage of society."[10] Since neither the love of husband and wife, or parent and child, is natural, then neither are the moral duties that arise from marriage and childbearing. (Rousseau added, with more than a little hint of autobiography, that the moral element of love is an artificial sentiment "extolled with much skill and care by women in order to establish their ascendancy and make dominant the sex that ought to obey."[11])

Had he stopped here, Rousseau would be celebrated merely as the father of the nineteenth-century randy intellectual rogue who lured naïve high-society women into believing a philosophy that made them his willing sexual prey. "Sex is natural. The chains of morality are not. Madam, let us throw off these shackles and recover our lost innocence!"

Such is true, but because Rousseau was a profound thinker, the damage goes far deeper. Not just sexual morality, but all morality was unnatural. For "men in that [primitive] state" were entirely amoral: as they did not have "among themselves any kind of moral relationship or known duties, they could be neither good nor evil, and had neither vices nor virtues."[12] Morality is therefore purely artificial. It develops only with society. Because society itself is not natural, neither is morality. "Savages are not evil," Rousseau asserts, "precisely because they do not know what it is to be good."[13]

But society is not just unnatural; it's actually bad. As Rousseau made clear in his *First Discourse*, the development of society—the development of the human being beyond mere isolated, animal existence—constitutes man's fall from idyllic, original, natural happiness into the morbid, vicious, entangling miseries of civilization, a tragic descent from natural freedom to artificial servitude. "Everyone must see," says Rousseau, "that...the bonds of servitude are formed only from the mutual dependence of men and the reciprocal needs that unite them." But in the state of nature, each man is entirely independent. The artificial chains of society "did not exist in the state of nature," therefore, "each man there" was "free of the yoke."[14]

We are not far from Marx and Engel's famous cry that closes the *Communist Manifesto*: "The communists disdain to conceal their views and aims. They openly declare that their ends can be attained only by the forcible overthrow of all existing social conditions. Let the ruling classes tremble at a communistic revolution. The proletarians have nothing to lose but their chains. They have a world to win. WORKINGMEN OF ALL COUNTRIES, UNITE!"[15]

There are, of course, important differences with Marx. Rousseau believed that because the advance of civilization (including the advance of technology, i.e., "the arts") caused our misery, then the only way to progress was to go backward, to recreate as best one could the condition of the undeveloped human animal, shaking off the artificial chains of society and returning to the purity of nature. For Marx and Engels, by contrast, the progressive conquering of nature and the stages of society that arise from it lead forward to a peaceful, communistic utopia, where technology provides an Edenic existence in which no one has to labor. Rousseau and Marx lead in opposite directions, one back and the other forward. What for Rousseau was a sign of decay became for Marx a sign of progress.

That having been said, Rousseau is still the father of Marxist thought, although we'll have to work a bit to show the connections. In the beginning, the man-animal owned nothing, Rousseau assures us. He had no idea of property because he had no idea of anything. He was entirely non-rational. His soul, "agitated by nothing," was "given over to the sole sentiment of its present existence without any idea of the future." He was blissfully living a life of "pure sensations."[16] He ate when he was hungry, slept when he was tired, and had duty-free sex when the mood struck him. In this original state, so Rousseau claims, there were plenty of acorns and apples for everyone. No thing belonged to anyone; nobody belonged to anyone. Each did as he wished, and since he wished for so little, there were no conflicts and no anxious toiling.

Things would have gone on this way indefinitely if not for a "first revolution." Some fool got it into his head to build a hut, and even worse, instead of running off after he'd conquered a woman, he invited her into his shelter. This "produced the establishment and differentiation of families," and "a sort of property," a distinction of mine and thine that never existed.[17] Things slid quickly downhill from there. Whereas the natural man was originally free, he became unnaturally tied down to a place and a family. As more families gathered, divisions of labor arose, allowing for the creation of both necessities and luxuries and assuring social interdependence.

At this point, the decline of man is already well on its way. The first revolution brings both virtue and vice. In the state of nature, sexual fidelity did not exist. But when a woman is labeled as one man's own, adultery is created where before was sexual freedom. From luxury come dissipation and vice. No one was a glutton before a surplus of food existed. From possession comes crime. No one could steal before there was a concept of ownership, and there was no ownership prior to the doleful invention of architecture and agriculture. From interdependence came inequality. All were equal when there were no distinctions based on labor, ownership, or comparison.

It would seem, then, that claiming something as one's own—private property—is the origin of all human misery and (to recall the title of Rousseau's treatise) of all inequality:

> The first person who, having fenced off a plot of ground, took it into his head to say *this is mine* and found people simple enough to believe him, was the true founder of civil society. What crimes, wars, murders, what miseries and horrors would the human race have been spared by someone who, uprooting the stakes or filling in the ditch, had shouted to his fellow-men: Beware of listening to this impostor; you are lost if you forget that the fruits belong to all and the earth to no one![18]

The implications of all this were picked up by Marx and Engels. Private property is unnatural and hence not good. All human conflict is caused by considering something as one's own (including one's own wife or children—note how many communists espoused free love and disparaged the family). The evils only get worse as the entanglements progress. Private property originates in, and is magnified by, division of labor; division of labor sets up unnatural social inequality that advances with technological progress. Thus, freedom from "crimes, wars, murders,... miseries and horrors" will end only if someone forcibly uproots the stakes of private property and drives them into the hearts of the owners. Communism!

The main difference between Rousseau and Marx is that Marx thought technology could ultimately provide the kind of idleness and plenty that Rousseau identified only with our original condition. Marx therefore believed that human progress through the various developmental historical stages could bring us (after the final cataclysmic revolution) to a condition of equality and property-free communism.

Marx was not Rousseau's only revolutionary child. Rousseau is perhaps more famous for spawning a different revolution, the French Revolution, and a closer look at his account of civil society shows us why. As we might have guessed from what's been said above, Rousseau believed that the inequalities of private property (and the consequent distinction between rich and poor) precede the explicit erection of civil society. Some guys in huts work harder; they get more land; their crops flourish; their animals multiply. Others are lazier, or stricken with bad luck, or foolish enough to choose some kind of labor that provides only moderate means. Population increases; society grows; the haves have more, the have-lesses have less. The gap between rich and poor grows accordingly.

Mere society is transformed into civil society when the few rich realize that the many poor could easily band together and overthrow them. They come up with a brilliant scheme. "Let us unite," say the rich charlatans to the poor fools, "to protect the weak from oppression, restrain the ambitious, and secure for everyone the possession of what belongs to him. Let us institute regulations of justice and peace to which all are obliged to conform."[19] What the rich really mean is, "Let us have laws, and the arms to enforce them, so that I may keep my riches." And so the poor fools were fooled, laments Rousseau:

> All ran to meet their chains thinking they secured their free-dom.... Such was ... the origin of society and laws, which gave new fetters to the weak and new forces to the rich, destroyed nat-ural freedom for all time, established forever the law of property and inequality, changed a clever usurpation into an irrevocable right, and for the profit of a few ambitious men henceforth sub-jected the whole human race to work, servitude, and misery.[20]

As civil society is based on injustice and law is merely a tool for the rich to keep their riches, then rebellion of the have-nots is always justified. They have nothing to lose but their chains. Voilà, the French Revolution ... and we are also back to Marx.

Let us count up the evils we should lay at Rousseau's door with his *Discourse on the Origin and Foundations of Inequality among Men.* We have seen the connections to Marx, and so we'll put off until the next chapter a further discussion of the evils of Marxism. But paving the way for the juggernaut of communism is not Rousseau's only evil.

Rousseau corrupted our imagination in a very profound way. Much of how we act, what we desire, what we consider true and false, real and unreal, is formed according to an image we have of what we think human beings really are and what we believe our place in nature to be. If we imagine ourselves to be truly at home in a dense, primeval forest, we shall never be at home anywhere else. If we imagine that sexual paradise consists in the carefree satisfaction of any sexual whim, then marriage and sexual morality will seem unnatural fetters on our desires. If we think that heaven on earth would be happy isolation, then (to quote ignominious French philosopher Jean-Paul Sartre) hell is other people.

We moderns live, in no small part, within Rousseau's imagination; to put it another way, we might say we have been made in the image of Rousseau. Modern man has discarded the idea that he is fashioned in the image of God, that he is to love his wife as himself, and that he should regard his children as precious miracles bearing his and his wife's image.

Instead, he accepts Rousseau's myth that he is a man-animal who would be happier if he left women with the same careless conscience as a rutting beast of the field, cast his children behind him to be tended by chance, and spent his days on his own satisfactions, living a life of "pure sensations." Beer, sports, television, movies, video games, iPods, the Internet, sex, sleep.

This is no harmless man-animal. It is a sad truth that human beings remake their societies according to the image of humanity they fashion for themselves. And so it is no accident that modern man-animals troll for sexual prey, convincing women that paradise is sex without strings and making institutions and laws for the disposal of children. We have become Rousseaus.

Despite Rousseau's grandiose praise of Roman virtue, he had a string of mistresses, some married, some not. He sired five children with one of them, Thérèse Levasseur, with whom he lived for more than twenty-five years and whom he treated as a mere maid (she delivered his torrid letters to other mistresses). Rousseau abandoned all five children to the Hôpital des Enfants-Trouvés, a foundling home where the conditions were so deplorable that their deaths were all but certain. What moral struggle did he undergo? In his own words, describing the first abandonment, he seems to undergo no more struggle than his fictional man-animal:

> I made up my mind cheerfully and without the least scruples, and the only ones I had to overcome were those of Thérèse. I had the greatest difficulty in the world getting her to accept this means of preserving her honor. Her mother, who feared the inconvenience of a brat, came to my aid, and she allowed herself to be overcome. A discreet and trustworthy midwife...was chosen...and when Thérèse's time came, she was taken there by her mother for the birth....He [the baby] was then deposited by the midwife at the Enfants-Trouvés office in the way that was customary. The following year there came the same inconvenience and the same expedients....I didn't reflect any further, and the mother didn't approve any more fully; she groaned but obeyed.[21]

This vicious but nonchalant assault on parenthood has been repeated too many times by the Rousseaus of our own day for us to add any further comment.

As with Hobbes, we see again the power of fiction. Rousseau's account of natural man was no more real than Hobbes's, but following the same pattern, once it became the accepted story of human origins, it thereby exercised the power of a self-fulfilling prophecy. In imagining Rousseau to be right, we have become what Rousseau imagined.

Part II
Ten Big Screw-Ups

CHAPTER FIVE

The Manifesto of the Communist Party (1848)

*"The history of all hitherto existing society
is the history of class struggle...."*

Karl Marx (1818–1883) and

Friedrich Engels (1820–1895)

NEVER HAVE SO FEW PAGES DONE SO MUCH DAMAGE. THE DAMAGE
has for the most part already been accomplished, and Marxism
itself (outside China) mainly stirs papers at academic conferences.
But communism offered one heck of a lesson. On body count
alone, *The Communist Manifesto* could win the award for the most
malicious book ever written. Now that we have more accurate cal-
culations of corpses—perhaps upwards of 100,000,000—even the
tenured Marxists are a bit squeamish about tooting the *Manifesto* as
a horn of plenty.

But as it has obviously failed so miserably, we must ask why it
succeeded so magnificently. What is it about Marx's grand vision
that inspired his disciples to clamber up the pile of corpses to have
a better look?

Before beginning, however, I must address an offensive criticism of the approach I'm going to take. I mean "offensive" in both senses, as if the best defense were merely to be offensive. Francis Wheen, in his otherwise fine biography of Marx, sets off sailing with the remark that, "Only a fool could hold Marx responsible for the Gulag; but there is, alas, a ready supply of fools.... Should philosophers be blamed for any and every subsequent mutilation of their ideas?"[1]

We assume from his rhetorical tone that our answer must be: "of course not!" but that would reveal dangerous ignorance of one of philosophy's most profound questions. That question—"should philosophers be blamed for any and every subsequent mutilation of their ideas?"—was near and dear to the three greatest philosophers who ever lived: Socrates, Plato, and Aristotle. It is not a fool's question; it was asked by Plato and Aristotle when the disciples of Socrates began to gravitate toward the support of political tyranny.

One might even say that one of the great differences between ancient and modern philosophy is that ancient philosophy takes this question with the utmost seriousness and modern philosophy dismisses it as foolish. Being a partisan of the ancients, I suggest that if Marx himself had attended to this question, Marxism's corpse count might have been considerably lower.

Perhaps, like some others, Wheen is assuming that philosophy isn't dangerous (another modern error!) because it is merely a thought in someone's head or a word on some book's page. Sticks and stones can break our bones but words can never harm us—that kind of thing. It is for this reason, I think, that Wheen puts the matter so abstractly, speaking of "philosophers" in a general way and not about the particular philosophy under consideration. If Lenin, Stalin, Mao, Pol Pot, and other professing Marxists were responsible for such egregious mutilations of humanity, then it is certainly legitimate—and even morally mandatory—to ask what is it about their master's words that inspired them to such epic crimes. One would have to be a fool to ignore such an inquiry.

Moreover, the *Manifesto of the Communist Party* was no mere philosophical theory; it was a call to political action: "A specter is haunting Europe—the specter of communism.... It is high time that communists should openly, in the face of the whole world, publish their views, their aims, their tendencies, and meet this nursery tale of the specter of communism with a Manifesto of the party itself."[2] Karl Marx, the primary author of the *Manifesto*, penned it for the Communist League in January 1848, five months shy of his thirtieth birthday. He was a supremely self-assured revolutionary whose characteristic traits were intelligence, political inexperience, and most prominent of all, an unconquerable desire to press his arguments upon all detractors, especially his fellow communists.

Marx didn't invent communism, nor was he the only one agitating for revolutionary changes at the midpoint of the nineteenth century. But he was, as Engels himself admitted, a dictator of any organization of which he was a part, and so he put his stamp down hard on the subsequent development of communism in Europe. Here is a revealing description by one Carl Schurz, who witnessed Marx in full plumage:

> I have never seen a man whose bearing was so provoking and intolerable. To no opinion which differed from his own did he accord the honour of even condescending consideration. Everyone who contradicted him he treated with abject contempt; every argument that he did not like he answered either with biting scorn at the unfathomable ignorance that had prompted it, or with opprobrious aspersions upon the motives of him who

had advanced it....he denounced everyone who dared to oppose his opinion.[3]

It is no wonder that there were only eleven mourners at Marx's funeral (not counting the corpse).

We mention these traits of Marx because they illuminate the essence of Marxism. It is an ideology fashioned according to a man's image, and forced on history with all the uncompromising power a grand theory can muster when it is disburdened of the possibility of contradiction from the facts. It is a theory full of youthful zeal in the very worst sense.

Long ago, Aristotle warned that young men are incapable of listening to lectures on political philosophy because they are doubly disadvantaged: they are overflowing with enthusiasm for changing the world, and this trait is all the more dangerous because they have so little knowledge of it. To them, everything seems possible, so they are especially prone to latching on to overly cerebral, utopian political schemes that fix every single problem in short order. That is why—if we recall our words above about philosophers being blamed for their ideas—Aristotle did not follow Socrates in his habit of speaking philosophically about politics with the young. Too many of Socrates' young protégés ended up endorsing tyranny. Marxism represents a peculiarly modern kind of tyranny: the tyranny of an idea over reality.

Marx's sidekick, Friedrich Engels, who was about two years younger than Marx, wrote the first draft of the *Manifesto*, but Marx put his decisive impress on communism's most famous document. The central ill of the *Manifesto* is its assumption of what came to be called historical materialism, which is linked to Marxism's atheism. Both Marx and Engels were atheists, and atheists don't like bothersome spiritual things. Therefore, they disallow them from existing and count on everything being purely material. That makes things very simple. Simplicity of a sort can be a kind of virtue. But the simplicity of Marxist reductionist materialism is a dreadful vice precisely because it ignores the complexity of the very things it professes to explain: human beings and human history.

Let us begin with its most famous statement: "The history of all hitherto existing society is the history of class struggle."[4] If you had read a fair amount of history (not written by a Marxist historian), your reasonable response might be something like this: well, Karl, certainly understanding the dynamics between social classes helps us to appreciate a significant part of each society's history, but there are a multitude of other aspects of human social life that defy so simple a formula. We should be wary of such a generalization if for no other reason than that the existence of different classes in any particular society has a host of complex causes. The intellectual aspects of culture, for example, seem to have little to do with the existence of, or struggle between, social classes.

Such comments, Marx would shoot back, are "not deserving of serious examination."

Really? Dare I ask why not?

"Does it require deep intuition to comprehend that man's ideas, views, and conceptions, in one word, man's consciousness, change with every change in the condition of his material existence, in his social relations, and in his social life?"

But, Karl...

"What else does the history of ideas prove than that intellectual production changes its character in proportion as material production is changed? The ruling ideas of each age have ever been the ideas of its ruling class."

Yes, well, I can see a certain...

"The history of all past society has consisted in the development of class antagonisms, antagonisms that assumed different forms at different epochs."

As I said, while class distinctions are important...

"But whatever form they may have taken, one fact is common to all past ages, viz., the exploitation of one part of society by the other."

Hold on there! Even you must admit that there are certainly other things all societies have in common besides some kind of exploitation. What about the desire for justice, the love between man and woman, the institution of marriage, the...

"No wonder...the social consciousness of past ages, despite all the multiplicity and variety it displays, moves within certain common forms, or general ideas, which cannot completely vanish except with the total disappearance of class antagonisms."

Come again? The disappearance of justice, love, marriage? That's what communism will give us—along with snatching up everybody's property?

"The communist revolution is the most radical rupture with traditional property relations; no wonder that its development involves the most radical rupture with traditional ideas....In place of the old bourgeois society, with its classes and class antagonisms, we shall have an association in which the free development of each is the condition for the free development of all."[5]

So flows the torrent from Marx's pen, battering opponents with abstractions rather than replying in detail to objections. If you disagree with him, then you are worse than an idiot; your very disagreement proves his thesis. Because all ideas are merely the reflections of social class, then the only reason you could have for disagreeing with Marx is that your head is filled with the ideas of the "old bourgeois society," the capitalist class that is oppressing the working class. You are then an obstacle to be eliminated by the proletarian revolution rather than a legitimate objection to be answered by reason.

If you've never encountered a Marxist, or read Marx himself, all of this heaping flow of abstractions probably makes little sense. So for the benefit of clarity, let's pick his argument apart and look at its assumptions.

We begin with the most important assumption, which we've already noted. Marx was an atheist and a materialist. The two go together; the denial of spiritual entities means the affirmation of all reality as purely material. What, then, is a human being? He is an animal that, like every other animal, must provide for his own material well-being. As human beings are furless animals with paltry claws and less than menacing teeth, they need to go much further than other animals in having to labor to produce things for their own sustenance and protection. The more complex the society and the more diverse the things it produces, the more complex is the division of labor that produces them. Recalling Rousseau, labor involves the removal of what is common to what is private, and hence arises private property.

Furthermore, the production of food, clothing, shelter, and methods of protection takes different forms or modes—say, in an agricultural society based on a hillside versus a fishing-based community by a seaside. Therefore, different societies have different modes of production that are manifested in the structure of their respective division of labor. We can even see how this division would manifest itself in distinct social classes—the rulers, the warriors, the landed gentry, the shopkeepers, the farmers, the artisans, and so on. Some would own more property or have more money than others, and some might indeed have little or no property or money. And we can even see that a certain amount of antagonism between the classes might arise, more in some societies, less in others.

Nothing particularly controversial or Marxist about what I've just said; in fact, Plato and Aristotle have quite profound and decidedly non-Marxist philosophical arguments based on the divisions of labor in society.[6] What keeps Marx from similar profundity is his devotion to materialistic simplicity and revolutionary utopianism.

In regard to materialistic simplicity, Marx made the fundamental error of confusing an important aspect of something with its entirety. Bulls have horns, but they are not merely life-support systems for their formidable headgear. Likewise, human beings need food, clothing, and shelter, yet they are not merely food-clothing-shelter producers. They have souls that long for truth, beauty, and happiness, a longing that transcends mere animal existence. Marx denies this. Since, for him, human beings are only material beings, then they are entirely defined by their material needs and desires, and hence by their various modes of producing food, clothing, shelter, and other material goods.

If we might indulge in Marx's passion for simplicity, we could put his entire argument in a slogan: "You are what you produce." This includes the ideas you produce. That is, human ideas are one more product of human labor, and Marx believes they are decided by a society's modes of production. In a fishing village, the language, laws, and customs, the notions of rights and privileges, the morality and mores will all be determined by its occupations—fishing, fish-packing, shipping. The same is true for culture. The focus of these villagers' art will be the sea and its bounty. They will sing songs about fishing, tell stories about great catches, and their proverbs will be tied to lessons learned at sea. Above all, their notions of the divine will be taken from their way of life, so that just as Hebrew goatherds and warriors spoke of a Great Shepherd-

Warrior in the sky, the fishing community will imagine a Neptunesque deity.

That's about as far as I can go in making this aspect of Marx's argument plausible. Obviously he espouses a radical relativism of morality, culture, and religion, but how is this radical relativism revolutionary? Why is history driving toward the grand conclusion of communism, rather than being merely a chronicle of the endless successions of various cultures, each self-contained and defined by its peculiar mode of production and hence way of life?

Now we are entering the core of Marxism. We accused Marx of being too abstract, of not attending to the real particularities of the evidence. We stand by that accusation, but add an explanation to avoid the obvious retort, "You haven't read much Marx beyond the *Communist Manifesto*, or you would have run into his excruciatingly detailed historical-economic analyses, such as in *Das Kapital.*"

To answer this reasonable charge, let's use an appropriate illustration to demonstrate both the revolutionary core and the central error of Marx's approach. Imagine if I were studying the family and focused in particular on families in which there were serious conflicts between parents and children. From this I concluded that the dynamic governing all families as families was "intergenerational conflict expressed in power relations of age-related dominance and rebellion." As it turns out, I also happened to live in a time in which the breakdown of the family was prominent, so that I was able to gather plenty of evidence for my conclusion that the dynamic governing families was intergenerational conflict.

Then, fired by the success of my thesis, I turned to history and found that in whatever society I looked, there were families consisting (lo and behold!) of parents and children, older and younger generations, and that there were signs of conflict, although not nearly as severe. From this I gather that because intergenerational conflict has grown alarmingly over the generations, there must be an overall historical trend grinding to an inevitable historical conclusion: the final rebellion of all children, resulting in the abolition of the family.

Note: I would indeed have a lot of very particular evidence, but my evidence, however detailed, would be warped in two ways. First, I have abstracted one aspect of the family, intergenerational conflict (taken largely from the example of unhappy families), leaving behind a significant number of other aspects that in healthy, happy families would be considered far more important. Second, I have leapt to the conclusion that the institution of the family will disappear, and that as a result all conflict will also disappear. But the "evidence" leads to this conclusion only because it has been set up that way—that is, by abstracting only certain "facts" about the family from the past and present, imposing an abstract schema upon history as a whole using these cherry-picked facts, and then positing as the end goal an abstract, never-before-experienced, utopian condition of family-lessness. And by "utopian" here, we don't mean "really good, yet very difficult to achieve" but "impossible, and hence entirely destructive if one tries to achieve it."

If we now move from our illustration to Marx's thesis, we see that much the same confusion by abstraction exists, but with a bit of added complexity. Marx happened to live at a time when the brutalities of industrialism were painfully evident. Many industrialists were getting richer and richer and seemed to use up their laborers like expendable tools. To give one example (from *Das Kapital*), Marx cites various European and American child labor laws from the first half of the nineteenth century that had to be passed as humanitarian measures to limit the number of hours children were being allowed or forced to work. "No child under twelve years of age shall be employed in any manufacturing establishment more than ten hours in one day," states the law of Massachusetts. How many hours were they working before this humanitarian legislation? Marx includes many vivid descriptions of the deplorable and dangerous living and working conditions of laborers—just as other reformers like Charles Dickens and Lord Shaftsbury did. Obviously, these conditions caused animosity between the industrialists (or capitalists or the bourgeoisie, as Marx variously calls them) and the workers (or proletariat).

But Marx drew several related, erroneous conclusions. The first was that all history is the story of class conflict. Given this assumption, he then views every aspect of society through his class warfare goggles, including the family itself, and so history really is grinding toward the abolition of the family as well. In the *Manifesto* Marx fires a rhetorical tirade against those who warn that communism will abolish the family along with private property. "Abolition of the family! Even the most radical [bourgeois thinkers] flare up at this infamous proposal of the communists," he retorts. But what these detractors mean by "family," he thunders, is only the "bourgeois family," the family as defined by the capitalist class. His rant continues:

> On what foundation is the present family, the bourgeois family, based? On capital, on private gain. In its completely developed form this family exists only among the bourgeoisie. But this state of things finds its complement in the practical absence of the family among the proletarians [because they work all their waking hours in factories, and hence are only together for a few hours of sleep], and in public prostitution.
>
> The bourgeois family will vanish as a matter of course when its complement [the proletarian family] vanishes, and both will vanish with the vanishing of capital....

The bourgeois claptrap about the family...about the hallowed co-relation of parent and child, becomes all the more disgusting, the more, by the action of modern industry, all family ties among the proletarians are torn asunder and their children transformed into simple articles of commerce and instruments of labor.

"But you communists would introduce community of women," screams the whole bourgeoisie in chorus.

...nothing is more ridiculous than the virtuous indignation of our bourgeois at the community of women which, they pretend, is openly and officially established by the communists. The communists have no need to introduce community of women; it has existed almost from time immemorial.

Our bourgeois, not content with having the wives and daughters of their proletarians at their disposal, not to speak of common prostitutes, take the greatest pleasure in seducing each other's wives.

Bourgeois marriage is in reality a system of wives in common and thus, at the most, what the communists might possibly be reproached with is that they desire to introduce, in substitution for a hypocritically concealed, an openly legalized community of women.[7]

So Marx answers the charge with the counter-charge: you bourgeois billygoats have already abolished the family! But he doesn't explain how society will get along without the family, which would seem to be the first and most natural institution. Moreover, he is beholden to an obvious fallacy—that all members of a class necessarily act in a particular way. Could it really be that (to give Engels's explanatory definition) "the class of modern capitalists, owners of the means of social production and employers of wage labor" were to a man leaping from the beds of their female workers to the beds of their confreres in capitalism, stopping to rest only in the arms of prostitutes? Perhaps Marx had a bad example all too close to home: bourgeois businessman Engels, who worked in his father's textile mill to support the revolution, was a notorious bed-hopper.

All delicious irony aside, this very kind of ideological illogic— some capitalists are womanizers, therefore, all capitalists as capitalists are tending toward the state of absolute womanizing, which represents the entire historical destruction of marriage—drives the engine of Marx's revolution.

We find this same kind of specious reasoning on every level. Some or many capitalists at this time abuse their laborers, treating them like human machines; therefore, all capitalists (i.e., anyone who owns a business and employs laborers) are irretrievably and irremediably tending toward the state of absolute oppression of laborers, a point where laborers will have nothing to lose but their chains. When they throw off their chains (and eliminate the bourgeoisie), they will discover themselves to be the only class left in a classless society. As industrial capitalism has entirely conquered nature, there is no more need for creating new class distinctions based on the mode of production. "In place of the old bourgeois society, with its classes and class antagonisms, we shall have an association in which the free development of each is the condition for the free development of all."

If we think back over Rousseau, we realize that Marx merely turned Rousseau on his head. Rousseau put an entirely fictional state of nature at the beginning of human history, a state in which there was magically no conflict, no private property, plenty for everyone, no family ties, and free sexual access to any woman.

Marx puts his entirely fictional state of frictionless bliss at the end, just beyond the great revolutionary conflagration.

We can see at this point why Marx's engine of revolution left its tracks so littered with corpses. Marx envisioned a misty and impossible goal and set it just beyond the reach of his devotees who were desperate enough (severely oppressed laborers) or foolish enough (intellectuals in the worst sense, like himself) to believe the fantasy as fact.

Precisely because the goal is both misty and impossible—that is, utopian—and because it is described as being just over the horizon, Marxists used the carrot of Marxist paradise as a stick to beat down all opposition. According to Marx, the fulfillment of the communist dream requires the disappearance of an entirely corrupt class. There is no moral blame attached to the revolutionaries who exterminate this class, and there is certainly no God to keep accounts. So it's no surprise that communism advanced by epic brutality. Such is the danger of a bad idea.

A final flourish of irony. The actual experience of Communist countries like China and the former Soviet Union demonstrates that once the proletariat and intellectuals get in charge, they turn out to be much more savage than the capitalists they displaced, snatching up every privilege within reach, enslaving a great part of the population for the "good of the revolution," and eliminating thousands or millions of those whose anti-revolutionary tendencies are deemed incurable.

What lesson to draw from all this? If Marxism proves anything, other than that the road to savagery is too often paved with gullibility as well as good intentions, it is the Christian doctrine of sin. To put it another way, if you really want to test whether there is an original and indelible fault that warps the human soul and is impossible to erase without divine intervention, then put power into the hands of those who, rejecting the existence of God as well as sin, wish to bring heaven to earth. We'll examine the first and greatest test with V. I. Lenin a few chapters hence, but we must suffer a few more fools in between.

CHAPTER SIX

Utilitarianism (1863)

"The ultimate end, with reference to and for the sake of which all other things are desirable, is an existence exempt as far as possible from pain, and as rich as possible in enjoyments. . . . "

John Stuart Mill (1806–1873)

THERE ARE MORE WAYS TO DESTROY THE HUMAN RACE THAN reducing it to a pile of smoldering corpses, and John Stuart Mill championed one of the most drab, utilitarianism. Even so sympathetic a scholar of Mill as Max Lerner felt compelled to say of *Utilitarianism* that Mill's "little book . . . leaves a trace of dust in the mouth."[1] For the unsympathetic, *Utilitarianism* leaves considerably more than a trace, perhaps enough to fill one's shoes and socks as well. Yet no one can gainsay the enormous influence that Mill's "little book" has had.

Perhaps something should be said of Mill's life so we can get an idea about where some of the dust came from. Mill's father, James, was a social reformer in the very worst sense, a man who, having been liberated from the "irrationalities" of faith, believed with immoderate intensity that the entire destiny and happiness of humanity rested upon his own efforts. A very dangerous man indeed.

James Mill came to his atheism (as his son reports) because "he found it impossible to believe that a world so full of evil was the work of an Author combining infinite power with perfect goodness and righteousness."[2] His "aversion to theism" was "of the same kind as that of Lucretius," the first-century BC Epicurean philosopher—an important fact, as we shall soon see.

Rather than giving his son a proper boyhood, James made his young son into an experiment, pressing him from the very earliest age to excel intellectually far beyond the capacities and emotional needs of a young boy. "I have no remembrance of the time when I began to learn Greek," relates Mill in his *Autobiography*. "I have been told that it was when I was three years old."[3] At a time when little John should have been on his father's lap reading stories about bunnies and elves, he was being ground through the Greek classics (his father mercilessly forbearing to teach him Latin until he was eight). In order not to have his "experiment" contaminated, the elder Mill kept young John from any contact with other children, especially other boys.

The result was predictable: John lost his boyhood reading works he could not possibly understand. Mill related in an early draft of his *Autobiography*, "My father's older children neither loved him nor with any warmth of affection anyone else." He also lacked "a really warm-hearted mother," so that he "grew up in the absence of love and in the presence of fear; and many and indelible are the effects of this bringing-up on my moral growth."[4]

These indelible effects are present in *Utilitarianism*, Mill's book on morality, a treatise as dry and loveless as his own youth. As with his father, the son meant well, and his all too influential work has been used as a paving-stone mold for all kinds of abominable good intentions since its publication in 1863.

Mill did not actually invent utilitarianism. That dubious honor belongs to Jeremy Bentham, a friend of his father's (and as John was disallowed any boyhood chums, somewhat his companion as well).

Bentham, another atheist, gave the world the notion that morality didn't need God; it needed only a good ledger to balance out pleasures and pains. Morality was merely a matter of calculating the greatest possible happiness for the greatest possible number. Bentham had the kind of self-confidence possible only in a man wholly unburdened by the nagging intricacies of intellectual, spiritual, and emotional depth and completely lacking in humility. Even John Stuart Mill himself was struck by Bentham's general woodenness of soul and unfitness for philosophy. Witness Mill's own words:

> Bentham's contempt, then, of all other schools of thinkers; his determination to create a philosophy wholly out of the materials furnished by his own mind, and by minds like his own; was his first disqualification as a philosopher. His second, was the incompleteness of his own mind as a representative of human nature. In many of the most natural and strongest feelings of human nature he had no sympathy; from many of its graver experiences he was altogether cut off; and the faculty by which one mind understands a mind different from itself, and throws itself into the feelings of that other mind, was denied him by his deficiency of Imagination.[5]

Not exactly what one looks for in a well-qualified philosophical mentor. Yet John would pick up the dreary flag of utilitarianism from Bentham and carry it forth as the philosophy of the future. "From the winter of 1821, when I first read Bentham," confessed Mill, "I had what might truly be called an object in life; to be a reformer of the world. My conception of my own happiness was entirely identified with this object."[6] This object was "Utility, or the Greatest Happiness Principle."[7]

The obvious question, then, is just exactly what utilitarianism is as Mill conceived it. The way to understand Mill's philosophy, paradoxically, is getting a good strong grip on what utilitarianism is not.

Imagine that human beings are created by an omniscient, omnipotent, and benevolent divine being as the very pinnacle of the visible world, so much so that human beings somehow bear the creator's image within them. Because they bear this image, they are fundamentally distinct from other kinds of living things. Thus, while they can kill other things (like weeds or groundhogs that invade their gardens, or cabbages and rabbits so they can eat them), they are forbidden by their creator to kill other human beings. Furthermore, as the act of sexual intercourse produces more human beings made in the image of the creator, sexuality is protected by certain restrictions that don't apply to other animals. In fact, there is a short list of commands handed out to human beings as a quick reference guide. The commands are simply meant to protect them from doing what violates their special status as creatures made in the image of the divine being, but this is only another way of saying that the commands lead them to share in the particular kind of happiness that the creator wished to bestow upon them as creatures made in his image. Sadly, these elevated and extraordinary creatures freely chose to act against the commands meant for their own good, and ever since there has been a kind of crack or fault line in the image, and human nature seems mysteriously distorted by the desire for self-destruction.

This is exactly what utilitarianism is not. Or, to put it another way, as Bentham and the Mills were all atheists, they could not rely upon such a theistic foundation for morality. They had to invent something to take its place.

This is trickier than it might sound at first, especially for these three because they were comfortable atheists. That is, they wanted all the moral benefits of Christianity, except without the Christianity part. They were the kind of self-assured chaps (so common in the nineteenth century) who took the fruits of centuries of Christian moral formation for granted even as they cheerfully chopped down the tree that had borne them. In consequence, they foolishly thought that because many Englishmen were generally solid and decent folk, moral solidity and decency could be counted on as standard equipment of human nature, and the whole religion thing could be thrown overboard as distracting nonsense. They made the entirely unforgivable assumption we have seen already in Rousseau: that there really is no such thing as original sin. Let us now look more closely at the not-God morality of utilitarianism and the confusions, contortions, and calamities it contrives.

As Mill himself admits, utilitarianism is not original, but is merely a revival of the ancient philosophy of Epicurus.[8] Epicurus was an atheist convinced that all the world's evils were caused by religion, and therefore religion needed to be swept like rubbish off the historical stage. To achieve this, he invented a purely materialist, spirit-proof cosmos, arguing that the universe existed from eternity (and hence needed no gods to create it), that everything arose from the random banging around of brute matter (Epicurus was the first evolutionist), and that consequently, human beings themselves were merely randomly contrived stacks of atoms that would eventually fall apart and blow away (so that, in not having an immortal, immaterial soul, they didn't have to worry about life after death or the vengeance of the divine).

Regarding morality, Epicurus argued that we don't need divine commands and sanctions. Instead, morality should be based on a very simple principle, what we might call the pleasure and pain principle (and it will become clear that Hobbes, like Mill after him, was also an Epicurean). As we are only physical things, there is no other meaning to *good* and *evil* than "this feels good" and "that feels bad." That is, Epicurus cut through all moral complexity with a double equation:

Good = Pleasure

Evil = Pain

This allows for a very simplified mode of moral reasoning— simple and wrong. The objections are obvious. For instance, adultery might be pleasurable for the adulterer, but what about the jilted spouse, or the children who are betrayed and confused when the marriage breaks up? The problems with Epicurus's morality are manifold. Nevertheless, Mill adopted Epicurus more or less whole hog—and his moral misreasoning is evident throughout *Utilitarianism.*

Let's begin with Mill's own statement of the "Greatest Happiness Principle," which underlies utilitarian moral philosophy (and in admirably succinct form exposes its foolishness):

According to the Greatest Happiness Principle...the ultimate end, with reference to and for the sake of which all other things are desirable (whether we are considering our own good or that of other people), is an existence exempt as far as possible from pain, and as rich as possible in enjoyments, both in point of quantity and quality; the test of quality, and the rule for measuring it against quantity, being the preference felt by those who in their opportunities of experience, to which must be added their habits of self-consciousness and self-observation, are best furnished with the means of comparison. This, being, according to the utilitarian opinion, the end of human action, is necessarily also the standard of morality, which may accordingly be defined, the rules and precepts for human conduct, by the observance of which an existence such as has been described might be, to the greatest extent possible, secured to all mankind; and not to them only, but, so far as the nature of things admits, to the whole sentient creation.[9]

If we unlace Mill's dry, tangled prose, we find that he is saying exactly what Epicurus said: morality's foundation is not God but pleasure and pain. But Mill adds to Epicurus two entirely necessary and entirely contradictory things.

The first thing Mill adds is the "test of quality." A moment's reflection reveals why this is necessary. The obvious rejoinder to Epicureanism (one made frequently against both Epicurus and Mill) is that it is a philosophy for pigs. Pigs also feel pleasure and pain. They like tasty grub, a wallow in the mud on a hot day, a fence to scratch where it itches, and a little porcine romance when the mood strikes. If happiness is simply equated with pleasure, then the Greatest Happiness Principle yields the conclusion that the perfect society would resemble that of well-fed hogs grunting about contentedly in a sty (or if we wish to maximize the intensity of pleasure to yield even greater happiness, the raging bacchanalia of an endless college fraternity party). Not a very elevated view of human morality, but entirely appropriate to the notion that morality should be rooted in pleasure and pain.

To counter this very obvious rejoinder, Mill insists that we must also take into account the pleasures of fine wine, classical music, the reading of philosophy by a fire, helping the downtrodden, disentangling Greek syntax to get a purer translation of Plato, and, of course, the peculiar tingling sensation one gets from being a "reformer of the world." But even here, another obvious rejoinder appears. If (as Bentham asserted) we must weigh pleasure against pleasure to calculate the greatest happiness for the greatest number, it would seem by sheer numbers that the pigs will win out. Pile up on one side of the scales the men who would rather guzzle cheap beer, have entirely unconstrained sex, and watch football for days at a time. On the other put the number who would rather parse a sentence in Greek and then go out and save hapless widows from penury. It doesn't take much practice in prophecy to see which way the scales will tip. Thus, according to the Greatest Happiness Principle, society should be set up, legally and morally, to maximize the pleasures of pigs, since their happiness/pleasure so drastically outweighs the pleasures of someone like Mill.

To avoid this, Mill claims that quality must judge quantity; that is, what constitutes happiness must be judged "by those who in their opportunities of experience, to which must be added their habits of self-consciousness and self-observation, are best furnished with the means of comparison." As we shall see, this is actually a long-winded way of saying "I, John Stuart Mill, and people just like me will judge and rank the pleasures, and hence determine how society will serve the Greatest Happiness Principle."

But now another problem arises. On the face of it, Mill would seem to be suggesting that the judge of morality must, as each pleasure (no matter how degraded) comes along, leap in with both feet to test the waters. Mill's atheism forces him to assert this ridiculous and unnatural position. Since there is no creator God and hence absolutely no moral commands written into nature, there are no intrinsically wrong actions. Consequently, the only way of judging things morally is by the actual experience of pleasure and pain. Our moral judge will have to experience both the staid and settled pleasures of marital fidelity and the wild pleasures of adultery; of sobriety and drunkenness; of playing chess and Jell-O wrestling; of reading papal encyclicals and pulp fiction; of fastidious vegetarianism and indiscriminate cannibalism. The hilarious thing is that Mill himself said as much:

> On a question which is the best worth having of two pleasures...
> the judgment of those who are qualified by knowledge of both,
> or, if they differ, that of the majority among them, must be admit-
> ted as final. And there needs be the less hesitation to accept this
> judgment respecting the quality of pleasures, since there is *no
> other tribunal* to be referred to even on the question of quantity.
> What means are there of determining which is the acuter of two
> pains, or the intenser of two pleasurable sensations, except the
> general suffrage of those who are familiar with both?... What is
> there to decide whether a particular pleasure is worth purchas-
> ing at the cost of a particular pain, except the feelings and judg-
> ment of the experienced?[10]

Even though Mill seems to be aware of the attendant problems and absurdities of his position in a vague way, he won't admit defeat, because he reserves to himself the right to a latent authoritarianism. Mill assumes that those who revel in sexual pleasure can judge moral matters if and only if they are also capable of experiencing, and indeed have experienced, the distinct pleasure of reading Plato in the original Greek. Something like this: as I, John Stuart Mill, and those like me, can read Greek and are capable of experiencing sexual excess, and you grubby fellows are not capable of reading Greek, then I and those like me must be the moral judges. The addition of quality, Mill thought, allowed utilitarianism to remain the morality of gentlemen rather than of pigs. It allows the pleasures of a refined human being to trump the animal pleasures of food, sex, and physical comfort.

But then Mill undoes it all by adding another perfectly logical but entirely contradictory element. He extends the principle of utility "so far as the nature of things admits, to the whole sentient creation." Why do such a strange and foolish thing? He had no choice. If morality is reduced to pleasure and pain, anything that experiences pleasure and pain must be included in the moral calculation. But here's the contradiction in the logic. Once we add the entire sentient population of every fish, fowl, reptile, amoeba, gorilla, and so forth, the task of ranking and balancing pleasures and pains becomes impossible. A sparrow cannot experience the pleasures of parsing Greek, but if Mill were to use that to deny "quality" to the sparrow's experience of pleasures, then the sparrow's advocate would reply that Mill cannot experience the pleasure of natural flight. Indeed, in the balance of all sentient beings, the sum of our human experience of pleasure and pain is negligible. Of course, modern animal rights activists say exactly this.

This brings us to another revealing defect, one that may have dawned on the reader. If we scratch down far enough in his argument, it becomes apparent that Mill's real belief was not in the principle of utility, but in himself and in his own direction of the moral life of human beings to achieve what he considered the greatest good for the greatest number. In modern politics we call this liberalism: the politicians and bureaucrats in Washington acting in the role of John Stuart Mill telling everyone else what to do. We can also call it playing God.

Playing God as a social reformer of humanity would seem to be a daunting task, unless (being an atheist) you are blissfully unfamiliar with original sin—as Mill clearly was, given his cheery view of how easy it would be to tidy up the mess of human history:

> Yet no one whose opinion deserves a moment's consideration can doubt that most of the great positive evils of the world are in themselves removable, and will, if human affairs continue to improve, be in the end reduced within narrow limits.... All the grand sources... of human suffering are in a great degree, many of them entirely, conquerable by human care and effort; and though their removal is grievously slow... yet every mind sufficiently intelligent and generous to bear a part, however small and unconspicuous, in the endeavour, will draw a noble enjoyment from the contest itself, which he would not for any bribe in the form of selfish indulgence consent to be without.[11]

These are the words of a dangerous madman. But even if we consider poverty an eradicable evil—as Mill did—no sane man can believe that the rich are always virtuous or that the prosperous would never be reduced to penury by gambling, philandering, and every other Epicurean excess. If curing disease (another evil named) could clear up the human condition, then the healthy would never steal, commit adultery, and drink their livers away. If education (a favorite utilitarian panacea) would make everyone an angel, then college seniors would do noticeably less libidinous and bibulous carousing than freshmen.

The problem is that Mill, being an atheist, did not see how deep evil runs. He believed his declaration of war on merely natural evils was enough to rid the world of all evil. Preventing heart attacks is all well and good, but there is more that ails the human heart. Mill, however, was too short-sighted to see it. He could not envision, for example, the most likely outcome of utilitarianism:

that it would lead to a society addicted to ever more intense, barbaric, and self-destructive pleasures, and that its members would be gibbering cowards in the face of even the smallest pains. Nor does he imagine that there might exist souls in a utilitarian society who long for something greater, something more noble, something truly more god-like than spending their days maximizing the physical pleasures of the multitude. Such a soul would soon boil over in contempt and vicious rebellion. That brings us to one of our next authors, Friedrich Nietzsche. But first, we must visit with another Englishman, Charles Darwin.

CHAPTER SEVEN

The Descent of Man
(1871)

*"At some future period, not very distant as measured
by centuries, the civilised races of man will almost
certainly exterminate and replace throughout the
world the savage races...."*

Charles Darwin (1809–1882)

READING CHARLES DARWIN'S *THE DESCENT OF MAN* FORCES ONE
to face an unpleasant truth: that if everything he said in his more
famous *Origin of Species* is true, then it quite logically follows that
human beings ought to ensure that the fit breed with abandon and
that the unfit are weeded out. Attempts to disengage Darwin from
the eugenics movement date from a bit after World War II, when
Hitler gave a bad name to survival of the fittest as applied to
human beings. But it is impossible to distance Darwin from eugenics: it's a straight logical shot from his evolutionary arguments.

Nearly everyone knows Darwin's argument about natural selection, put forth in his epoch-making *Origin of Species* (1859). Here it
is again, in all its simplicity:

As many more individuals of each species are born than can possibly survive; and as, consequently, there is a frequently recurring struggle for existence, it follows that any being, if it vary
however slightly in any manner profitable to itself, under the
complex and sometimes varying conditions of life, will have a
better chance of surviving, and thus be *naturally selected.* From the
strong principle of inheritance, any selected variety will tend to
propagate its new and modified form.[1]

Thus, survival of the fittest. The entire *Origin of Species* is an elab-
oration of this one statement (though the phrase "survival of the
fittest" doesn't appear in the first edition of the book; Darwin later
borrowed it from Herbert Spencer, who became an early and powerful advocate of social Darwinism). The strong—whether stronger
physically or simply better fitted to their environment—survive
and hence live on to breed more like themselves.

Now note what Darwin doesn't say (at least in the *Origin*). Imagine if the paragraph quoted above had been slightly altered:

As many more human beings are born than can possibly survive;
and as, consequently, there is a frequently recurring struggle for
existence, it follows that any human being, if he vary however
slightly in any manner profitable to himself, under the complex
and sometimes varying conditions of life, he will have a better
chance of surviving, and thus be *naturally selected.* From the strong
principle of inheritance, any selected men will tend to propagate
their new and modified form.

Of course, Darwin wrote no such thing in his *Origin of Species.*
He waited about a decade, and then put something very much like
it in his less famous but more infamous *Descent of Man.* Before we

dig in to that lamentable text and ferret out its gruesome implications, we ought to mull over the interesting omission of human beings from Darwin's discussion of evolution in the *Origin of Species.*

As anyone who has read the *Origin* cover to cover can attest, Darwin studiously avoids the obvious question: "Well, this is all very interesting, but since we human beings also vary—some of us are taller than others, some smarter, some faster, some blue-eyed and blond-haired, and so on—and we also breed just like animals, doesn't this all apply to us as well?"

Quite prudently (in the crass sense of prudence) Darwin avoided mixing human beings into his argument in the *Origin of Species.* He knew that if he did, his theory would be rejected. Evolution was already controversial enough. For some fifty years or more, it had been associated with political radicals, the kind of thing bandied about by French revolutionaries and gutter atheists. (Yes, you read that right. Contrary to popular opinion, Darwin did not "discover" evolution. It had wafted about radical circles for at least one, if not two centuries, before Darwin, and can be traced back to the ancient Greek philosopher Epicurus.[2]) But Darwin wasn't preaching to the radical choir. He wanted his theory to be heard by the more politically conservative bastions of England's scientific elite.

It was Darwin's own cousin, Francis Galton, who first elucidated the *Origin*'s obvious conclusions for human beings in a two-part article in *Macmillan's Magazine* in 1865, and then more completely in his book *Hereditary Genius* (1869). Darwin followed quickly with his own account, *The Descent of Man.* The obvious conclusion is eugenics. While Galton coined the term, Darwin provided the deep foundations and traced out the nasty implications.

Let us be clear about that. The pernicious aspect of Darwin's *Descent* is not the mapping of our ancestry to chimpanzees or gorillas. Much the same inference, whatever its ultimate merit, might have been made from watching rugby. The deep-down nastiness of the *Descent* is eugenic: the idea that the "survival of the fittest" should be *applied* to human beings. The emphasis is important. Eugenics is an applied science. It applies the science of breeding to human beings as if they were racehorses, or more accurately, farm animals. The best are allowed to breed; the worst (or "unfit") are eliminated. The Nazis would later apply this idea very effectively. As they saw it, natural selection is natural; nature favors the strong and picks off the weak. Society should not interfere with nature by artificially protecting the weak from destruction. Such charity is unnatural and hence unscientific. Instead, society should help natural selection with its work and wipe out the weak by even more efficient means. That is the science of eugenics.

That Darwin gave birth to this evil notion is not an abstract charge made by tenuous inferences from obscure footnotes. Behold the words of the man himself as he describes the baneful effects of civilized charity. Unlike us civilized folk, savages bow to the principle of survival of the fittest, and all the better for them:

> With savages, the weak in body or mind are soon eliminated; and those that survive commonly exhibit a vigorous state of health.... We civilised men, on the other hand, do our utmost to check the process of elimination; we build asylums for the imbecile, the maimed, and the sick; we institute poor-laws; and our medical men exert their utmost skill to save the life of every one to the last moment. There is reason to believe that vaccination has preserved thousands, who from a weak constitution would formerly have succumbed to small-pox. Thus the weak members of civilised societies propagate their kind. No one who has attended to the breeding of domestic animals will doubt that this

must be highly injurious to the race of man. It is surprising how soon a want of care, or care wrongly directed, leads to the degeneration of a domestic race; but excepting in the case of man himself, hardly any one is so ignorant as to allow his worst animals to breed.[3]

Darwin could hardly have been more direct. "Care wrongly directed" is causing the evolutionary downslide among the civilized:

If... various checks... do not prevent the reckless, the vicious and otherwise inferior members of society from increasing at a quicker rate than the better class of men, the nation will retrograde, as has occurred too often in the history of the world. We must remember that progress is no invariable rule.[4]

A slight but important historical detour at this point. Although your high school biology textbook undoubtedly had a short section on Darwin and was laced throughout with discussions of evolution, it probably left out Darwinism's eugenic implications. But such was not always the case. Witness this discussion from a high school biology text in use in 1917:

Improvement of Man.—If the stock of domesticated animals can be improved, it is not unfair to ask if the health and vigor of the future generations of men and women on the earth might not be improved by applying to them the laws of selection.

Eugenics.—When people marry there are certain things that the individual as well as the race should demand. The most important of these is freedom from germ diseases which might be handed down to the offspring. Tuberculosis, that dread white plague which is still responsible for almost one seventh of all deaths, epilepsy, and feeble-mindedness are handicaps which it is not only unfair but criminal to hand down to posterity. The science of being well born is called *eugenics*.[5]

The book goes on to warn students about the infamous Jukes family, whose prodigious mental and moral defects were passed on through even more prodigious breeding. Of the 480 descendants of the original genetically ill-starred pair, "33 were sexually immoral, 24 confirmed drunkards, 3 epileptics, and 143 feeble-minded."[6] The book continues:

Parasitism and Its Cost to Society.—Hundreds of families such as those described above exist to-day, spreading disease, immorality, and crime to all parts of this country. The cost to society of such families is very severe. Just as certain animals or plants become parasitic on other plants or animals, these families have become parasitic on society. They not only do harm to others by corrupting, stealing, or spreading disease, but they are actually protected and cared for by the state out of public money. Largely for them the poorhouse and the asylum exist. They take from society, but they give nothing in return. They are true parasites.

The Remedy.—If such people were lower animals, we would probably kill them off to prevent them from spreading. Humanity will not allow this, but we do have the remedy of separating the sexes in asylums or other places and in various ways preventing intermarriage and the possibilities of perpetuating such a low and degenerate race. Remedies of this sort have been tried successfully in Europe and are now meeting with success in this country.[7]

Until the last line, you probably thought you were reading a textbook written by proto-Nazi biologists, but such is not the case. The excerpts come from George William Hunter's *A Civic Biology.* Ring any bells? Hunter's book was the high school textbook at issue in the famous Scopes trial of 1925. It was the pro-evolution textbook that the forces of progress led by lawyer Clarence Darrow defended against the "booboisie" and William Jennings Bryan. Wouldn't those passages have sounded dandy coming out of the mouth of Spencer Tracy (playing the Clarence Darrow character) in that great Hollywood cinematic propaganda piece *Inherit the Wind?* Must have gotten cut.

Our point is that eugenic thinking was not something tacked on to Darwin by thuggish brownshirts in 1930s Germany. Rather, it was and is a direct implication drawn from Darwin's account of evolution, one that Darwin himself drew quite vividly in his *Descent of Man.* Furthermore, in the latter half of the nineteenth and first half of the twentieth century eugenics was popular not just in Germany but all over Europe and America. It was understood to be a legitimate inference from Darwin, because Darwin himself made the deduction, and so it was written into biology textbooks—even in America.

To be fair to Darwin, he did shrink back from suggesting direct extermination (as did Hunter's *A Civic Biology,* however reluctantly), but not because mercy was inherently good. After all, mercy was itself merely a by-product of blind evolutionary forces. According to Darwin, such charity was merely an "incidental result of the instinct of sympathy, which was originally acquired as part of the social instincts."[8]

To translate, Darwin believed that morality was neither natural nor God-given, but was itself the result of natural selection. Whatever actions, attitudes, or passions happened to contribute to the survival of an individual or group were naturally selected. The virtue of courage, for example, was naturally selected because in the struggle for existence the cowardly are wiped out right quick and the manly types live on to breed happily with the appreciative maidens. The same goes for sympathy. Because people who stick together can usually pummel natural loners, the "social instinct" is naturally selected, and the anti-social are cast out of the gene pool. Within the social instinct is a sub-trait, "sympathy." Sympathy makes us feel sad or uncomfortable at someone else's suffering or extermination. That's what keeps us from acting like savages. Somehow, somewhere sympathy contributed more to survival than savagery, and according to the great law of natural selection, "those communities, which included the greatest number of the most sympathetic members, would [therefore] flourish best and rear the greatest number of offspring."[9] So it was that sympathy spread, and won out over savagery. That's what makes it hard for the civilized folk to savagely eliminate the weak, even if natural selection would appear to call for it.

But we must remember that the trait of sympathy is not essentially good. It came from indifferent random genetic variations. It is no more moral than, say, red hair, blue eyes, or the Habsburg jaw. On Darwin's account, the things we call "moral" are simply traits that somehow contributed to our ancestors' survival. Oddly enough, Darwin asserted that we could not "check our sympathy, if so urged by hard reason, without deterioration in the noblest part of our nature." The evolutionary development of sympathy as a trait was, so to speak, worth the cost. I say "oddly enough" because evolution doesn't aim at any goal, such as nobility. Evolution aims at utility, that is, at the usefulness of particular traits under particular circumstances. When circumstances change, these same traits might actually prove harmful. Thus, even though sympathy may have helped one set of people cohere, it could actually become harmful to them when the load of "unfit" becomes so heavy that it weighs them down when they come into conflict with another set of people unburdened by the sympathy trait.

For whatever reason, Darwin was unwilling to bite his own bullet. "Hence we must bear without complaining," he wrote, with a melancholy sigh, "the undoubtedly bad effects of the weak surviving and propagating their kind." Yet, he suggested, at least "the weaker and inferior members of society" might keep from "marrying so freely as the sound," or even better, agree to "refraining from marriage" altogether.[10]

As anyone familiar with the history of the eugenics movement knows, Darwin's enchantment with sympathy was soon jettisoned as maladaptive, and hard reason prevailed. That doesn't mean that Darwin is off the hook, however. The reasoning behind eugenics, however hard, was quite in conformity with Darwin's principles, and it was done by some of the leading intellects of Europe and America.[11]

Darwin's eugenics had another interesting twist. We often hear of his antipathy toward slavery, a product of his latitudinarian, Whig (liberal) background, so we assume that he would be untainted by racism. Indeed, racism would seem to be quashed by the evolutionary spread of sympathy. In Darwin's own inspiring words:

[A]s man gradually advanced in intellectual power and was enabled to trace the more remote consequences of his actions; as he acquired sufficient knowledge to reject baneful customs and superstitions; as he regarded more and more not only the welfare but the happiness of his fellow-men; as from habit, following on beneficial experience, instruction, and example, his sympathies became more tender and widely diffused, so as to extend to the men of all races, to the imbecile, the maimed, and other useless members of society, and finally to the lower animals, so would the standard of his morality rise higher and higher.[12]

As cheerful as the ever-widening spread of the balm of sympathy sounds, there are two flies in the ointment. First, there are few moral concepts as slippery as sympathy. At best, it substitutes indiscriminate niceness for goodness in human affairs. (Niceness is nice, but even a thief can be polite.) At worst, it embraces indiscrimination itself, and erases all boundaries between human beings and every other living thing. In trying to treat every living thing as part of one moral whole, it ends up inverting the entire moral order and the natural order along with it. The outcome is the animal rights activist who, overflowing with sympathy for the chimpanzee, destroys medical research clinics.

The slipperiness of sympathy has its origin in the central feature of Darwin's *Descent of Man*: the assumption that human beings are just one more animal on the evolutionary spectrum. If we are just one more animal, and so-called "moral" traits are ultimately no more moral than any other evolved traits, then we obviously are not morally distinct from any other animal. Indeed, as Darwin argues in a number of passages, other animals have something like moral traits too, differing in degree, not in kind.

Either way—whether we are not moral, or animals are—the moral difference between human beings and other animals is blurred if not erased. Such is the result of extending the moral trait of "sympathy" to the lower animals. That is what has brought animal rights activists to the conclusion that if human beings have rights, animals have rights as well. The logic is simple enough:

sympathy is the most important moral trait; sympathy is feeling bad when others suffer; animals not only suffer, but show signs of having the trait of sympathy too; therefore, they are as moral as we are, and if human beings have rights, then so do other animals. (Oddly enough, one would think it would then follow that if we have moral faults, then animals have moral faults as well, but animal rights activists don't spread the wet blanket of moral blame over the rest of the animal kingdom. Not one of them ever stopped by my farm and protested how savagely our three roosters treated their hens. We gave up waiting for PETA, and out of sympathy for the hens, finally ate the roosters.)

A second fly in the ointment of sympathy comes from Darwin himself. Sympathy, in the Darwinian scheme, is just one of the variable effects of natural selection. Race is another. Human races are like different breeds of dogs. They are the result of divergent evolutionary developments. The distinct human races, Darwin informs us, are best considered "sub-species," that is, somewhere between the transition from distinct breed to distinct species.[13]

But for Darwin, evolution cannot stop there. As time passes, the difference between human races will lead to the evolution of entirely different species. This does not occur from the Chinaman turning into one species, while an Englishman and an African turn into others, but through the elimination of some races by other races according to survival of the fittest. It is a law of evolution that the most closely related species or sub-species are those most likely to come into conflict, and so, in a series of closely related species or sub-species stretched across a spectrum—say, A, B, C, D, E, F, G, H—the "middle" ones get knocked out in the struggle, and the two most distant and distinct (A and H) survive as the fittest. The same invariable law applies to human races as well, and we must remember that the human races themselves exist on a much wider evolutionary spectrum, along with gorillas, orangutans, chimpanzees, and so on.

Here comes the nasty part. Evolution is driven by competition, and competition brings extinction. Darwin notes, matter-of-factly, that "extinction follows chiefly from the competition of tribe with tribe, race with race.... When civilised nations come into contact with barbarians the struggle is short, except where a deadly climate gives its aid to the native race."[14] That is not a moral complaint; it is a detached scientific description uttered without angst. As the engine of evolution is never idle, it is also a prophecy:

> At some future period, not very distant as measured by centuries, the civilised races of man will almost certainly exterminate and replace throughout the world the savage races. At the same time the anthropomorphous [i.e., most human-looking] apes . . . will no doubt be exterminated. The break will then be rendered wider, for it will intervene between man in a more civilised state, as we may hope, than the Caucasian, and some ape as low as a baboon, instead of as at present between the negro or Australian and the gorilla.[15]

Get it? Ranking the human races, we find the Caucasian at top, and down at the bottom, dangling at the edge of humanity, "the negro or Australian" who is just an evolutionary hair's-breadth away from the anthropomorphous gorilla. In pushing for the über-Caucasian, evolution also exterminates all the "intermediate species," so that natural selection will do away with the negro, the aboriginal Australian, and the gorilla.

The problem with scientific prophecies, especially pseudo-scientific prophecies, is that they all too often are then taken to be destinies. It is no good holding up Darwin's account of sympathy as a way of trying to extricate him from blame for the harsh racial eugenics practiced by the harder-reasoning Nazis. Having read the *Descent of Man*, we can no longer claim that Darwin didn't intend the biological theory of evolution outlined in the *Origin of Species* to be applied to human beings. Nor can we brush his pernicious words away with a dismissive "He's just a man of his time." Darwin made his time—and as we shall see in later chapters, the time of those who followed him.

CHAPTER EIGHT

Beyond Good and Evil
(1886)

*"Christianity has been the most
calamitous kind of arrogance yet. . . . "*

Friedrich Nietzsche (1844–1900)

THE ONLY THING MOST PEOPLE KNOW ABOUT THE GERMAN philosopher Friedrich Nietzsche is that he proclaimed "God is dead." Or, by extension, they've heard the tiresome joke:

"God is dead."

—Nietzsche

"Nietzsche is dead."

—God

This doubtless gives some momentary comfort to religious believers that, in the end, mortality has the last say. But it is hardly a rebuttal of this most powerful of atheistic philosophers, nor is it a demonstration of the existence of God. To begin with, we are all going to die, theist and atheist alike, and our respective mortality is no proof or disproof of the caliber of our arguments. Secondly, while many know that Nietzsche said "God is dead," very, very few know what he meant. It was not a cry of triumph, but of despair uttered against an ever more trivial and dwindling civilization that Nietzsche thought was sapping humanity of all greatness, producing something just barely above the animal: the last man.

Indeed, in its first sustained exposition in Nietzsche's works, it is uttered by a "madman" who cries out, "Whither is God?...I will tell you. *We have killed him*—you and I. All of us are murderers.... Is there any up or down? Are we not straying as through an infinite nothing? Do we not feel the breath of empty space? Has it not become colder? Is not night continually closing in on us?...God is dead. God remains dead. And we have killed him."[1]

Nietzsche is that madman. And indeed, he died a madman, having grasped and then been torn apart by the terrible implications of his own words. Unlike most other atheists, Nietzsche was brutally honest about what atheism really meant, and that honesty ultimately cost him his sanity. No up or down; no good or evil; just sheer human will swimming in an indifferent, if not hostile, cosmos.

What all this means we shall soon see. But I want to assure the reader up front that there can be no easy rebuttal to Nietzsche's atheism precisely because it is a most profound atheism. The bestseller atheists around now (like Richard Dawkins, Christopher Hitchens, and Sam Harris) are pussycat atheists, not lions like Nietzsche who, if he were still around, would chew them up and spit them out in disgust.

That does not make Nietzsche a friend to religion. After all, he declared himself to be the Antichrist. But he was a savage enemy of all lukewarmness, all halfway housebuilding, whether done in the name of religion or irreligion. His most vicious words were aimed at liberal Christians who had dispensed with all the majesty and terror of Christianity and preached the wan humanitarianism of niceness and at liberal atheists (like John Stuart Mill) who had not recognized the real terror and ruthless majesty of atheism and likewise preached the wan humanitarianism of niceness. Niceness, howled Nietzsche, is what is left of goodness when it is drained of greatness.

I stress these points because there are now many so-called and self-proclaimed disciples of Nietzsche who smooth over his sharp points—even file them off completely—because they would seem to point directly and unambiguously to Hitler and Nazi Germany. They like his bold atheism—just as boys like to strike gallant poses as if they were really warriors—but shrink from the actual implications spelled out all too clearly by Nietzsche himself. They want all the benefits of not having a God looking over their shoulders exacting moral demands, but they also want a universe with moral structure (albeit one marked by convenience rather than rigor). They still want to condemn the crimes of Hitler as the greatest possible crimes.

But for Nietzsche, the greatest possible crimes are the very things needed to lift humanity out of its increasingly degraded state and into something grand and glorious. That is why he cries out that we—or more accurately, a few brave and singular souls—must go beyond good and evil. Nietzsche's present-day disciples miss precisely this sharpest of points: to go beyond belief in God is to go beyond good and evil. If one has not gone beyond good and evil, then one has not gone beyond belief in God.

We have arrived at the title of Nietzsche's famous work, *Beyond Good and Evil.* It is more exhortation than argument, so it is perhaps better to step back a little and make some sense of where Nietzsche ended up by surveying the ground we've already covered from Machiavelli to Mill.

As we have seen with Machiavelli, atheism was alive and well almost four centuries before Nietzsche. Much of the advice in *The*

Prince demanded that aspiring rulers shed all concerns about whether actions were considered good or evil and concentrate instead on whether actions were effective in putting a prince in power and keeping him there. Power was more important than moral distinctions. While Machiavelli avoided outright declarations of atheism, the kind of counsel he offered could only be given (and accepted) by someone who had long ago left religious beliefs behind. Already in Machiavelli, then, we have atheism wedded to an incipient notion of Nietzsche's famous will-to-power.

We also saw Hobbes set forth a view of nature that was entirely godless and amoral, a view of the universe that denied any natural, intrinsic good or evil. Instead, good and evil are only particular preferences, meaning merely "I like this; this brings me pleasure" and "I dislike this; this causes me pain." The person who can impose his likes and dislikes on everyone else thereby defines good and evil. Or if we might say it the other way around, behind any seemingly objective standard of good and evil lie the arbitrary, subjective preferences of someone in power. Hence the importance of religion: it allows one's arbitrary desires to masquerade as a god's.

Nor should we forget Darwin's contribution. Darwin did not so much deny morality as redefine it in terms of what contributed to the survival of the fittest. In Darwin's view, nature's elimination of the weak and crowning of the strong are what drives species upward. If the struggle for survival is relaxed, the upward-driving tension in the evolutionary bow dissipates. "We must remember," said Darwin, "that progress is no invariable rule."[2]

> Man, like every other animal, has no doubt advanced to his present high condition through a struggle for existence consequent on his rapid multiplication; and if he is to advance still higher he must remain subject to severe struggle. Otherwise he would soon

sink into indolence, and the more highly gifted men would not be more successful in the battle of life than the less gifted.[3]

What has climbed up through struggle might slip back down the evolutionary slope again. That's the bad news. But on the bright side, as human beings have been raised above the other animals by the struggle to survive, they may be raised even higher, transcending human nature to something—who knows?—as much above men as men are now above apes.

This strange hope rests in Darwin's very rejection of the belief that man is defined by God, for "the fact of his having thus risen" by evolution to where he is, "instead of having been aboriginally placed there" by God, "may give him hopes for a still higher destiny in the distant future."[4] Nietzsche takes up Darwin's hope for the self-creation of this creature-to-be, the *übermensch*, the over-man or super-man.

Finally we have John Stuart Mill's contribution. Nietzsche interpreted Mill's "greatest happiness for the greatest number" as a victory of the lowest, most animal-like pleasures over the most human and refined. Moreover, considered from a Darwinian perspective, utilitarianism leads to the "less gifted" swamping the gene pool, and hence brings about an evolutionary relapse wherein human nature recedes entirely into its animal origins. For Nietzsche and Darwin both, without pain there is no gain.

With Nietzsche, this was true not only in regard to the survival of the fittest, but even more important, to the flourishing of greatness in civilization: in art, architecture, music, philosophy. All human greatness demanded great suffering, harsh discipline, renunciation of comfort, courage against pain, and even cruelty in its use and elimination of the weak. Nietzsche cried out in disgust and defiance at "all these ways of thinking"—like "hedonism" or "utilitarianism"—"that measure the value of things in accordance with *pleasure* and *pain*":

> You want, if possible—and there is no more insane "if possible"—*to abolish suffering*? And we? It really seems that *we* would rather have it higher and worse than ever. Well-being as you understand it—that is no goal, that seems to us an *end*, a state that soon makes man ridiculous and contemptible—that makes his destruction *desirable.*
>
> The discipline of suffering, of *great* suffering—do you not know that only *this* discipline has created all enhancements of man so far? That tension of the soul in unhappiness which cultivates its strength, its shudders face to face with great ruin, its inventiveness and courage in enduring, persevering, interpreting, and exploiting suffering, and whatever has been granted to it of profundity, secret, mask, spirit, cunning, greatness—was it not granted to it through suffering, through the discipline of great suffering?[5]

"We should reconsider cruelty and open our eyes," chides Nietzsche. "Almost everything we call 'higher culture' is based on the spiritualization of cruelty, on its becoming more profound: this is my proposition." Breaking the four-minute mile demanded the superior abilities of Roger Bannister coupled with intense, painful training. Endless hours of excruciating self-denial went into Michelangelo's adornment of the Sistine Chapel. The glories of the pyramids were made possible by the relentless cruelty of slave labor. Such is the cost of all human greatness. It pays in the coin of pain, and hence greatness itself would be destroyed by maximizing pleasure and comfort and treating pain itself as simply evil.

If we keep all this in mind, we can better understand Nietzsche's *Beyond Good and Evil.* But we cannot get to the raging heart of it if we do not emphasize one thing more, something that has emerged in the above quotations: a deep, aristocratic contempt for mediocrity. This is a difficult and alien feeling for a democratic age to understand, but without some inkling of its natural source, we can neither understand Nietzsche nor guard against the ever-present danger his philosophy presents. Here are Nietzsche's own disdainful words as he further pommels the utilitarians:

> None of these ponderous herd animals...wants to know or even sense that "the general welfare" is no ideal, no goal, no remotely intelligible concept, but only an emetic—that what is fair for one *cannot* by any means for that reason alone also be fair for others; that the demand of one morality for all is detrimental for the higher men; in short, that there is an order of rank between man and man, hence also between morality and morality. They are a modest and thoroughly mediocre type of man, these utilitarian Englishmen.[6]

Nietzsche's view was that the utilitarians made mediocrity into a morality, a mediocrity aimed at the most animal-like, herd-like type of existence, a kind of "slave" morality that cared only for comfort and trivial pleasures and shrank from every harsh demand. But this goes against all that has, in the past, made man great, and so the trend must be reversed. There must be a revolution against the democratic, utilitarian spirit, the spirit that equalizes everything, thereby extinguishing the notion of greatness itself: "Every enhancement of the type 'man' has so far been the work of an aristocratic society—and it will be so again and again—a society that believes in the long ladder of an order of rank and differences in value between man and man, and that needs slavery in some sense or other."[7] Nietzsche believed this to be simple historical fact:

> Let us admit to ourselves...how every higher culture on earth so far has *begun*. Human beings whose nature was still natural, barbarians in every terrible sense of the word, men of prey who were still in possession of unbroken strength of will and lust for power, hurled themselves upon weaker, more civilized, more peaceful races.... In the beginning [therefore], the noble caste was always the barbarian caste: their predominance did not lie mainly in physical strength but in strength of the soul—they were more *whole* human beings (which also means, at every level, "more whole beasts").[8]

This account of tribal warfare is, we should note, quite similar to Darwin's. In the upward evolution of man, the warpath is the path of progress, as Darwin makes clear in his *Descent of Man*. In fact, for Darwin war is the source of the evolutionary development of such noble virtues as courage:

> When two tribes of primeval man, living in the same country, came into competition, if the one tribe included...a greater number of courageous, sympathetic, and faithful members, who were always ready to warn each other of danger, to aid and defend each other, this tribe would without doubt succeed best and conquer the other. Let it be borne in mind how all-important, in the never-ceasing wars of savages, fidelity and courage must be.... A tribe possessing the above qualities in a high degree would spread and be victorious over other tribes; but in the course of time it would, judging from all past history, be in its turn overcome by some other and still more highly endowed

tribe. Thus the social and moral qualities would tend slowly to advance and be diffused throughout the world.[9]

The similarities between Darwin's account and Nietzsche's are obvious: all rising above the merely animal is caused by struggle, war, and the brutal elimination of the less fit by the stronger. Nietzsche believed this to be the core natural truth of aristocracy—that the better should rule over, and hence should use, the lesser. "The essential characteristic of a good and healthy aristocracy" is that it "accepts with a good conscience the sacrifice of untold human beings who, *for its sake*, must be reduced and lowered to incomplete human beings, to slaves, to instruments." The "fundamental faith" of aristocracies then, is that "society" exists for them, for their sake, so that all the lesser types who serve them in society exist "only as the foundation and scaffolding on which a choice type of being is able to raise itself to its higher task and to a higher state of being."[10] One cannot help but think of the Nazi's justification for enslaving the Slavs as "lower men."

The differences between Darwin's account and that of Nietzsche must also be noted. First, Darwin is trying to give an evolutionary account of the "moral" qualities that lead up to something very like English utilitarianism, in which sympathy for all suffering is the highest moral development of evolution, and Nietzsche regards such sympathy as destructive of evolution's forward march. That is, Nietzsche rightly sees that Darwin's praise of sympathy contradicts his own account of exactly what makes for evolutionary progress: "life itself is *essentially* appropriation, injury, overpowering of what is alien and weaker; suppression, hardness, imposition of one's own forms, incorporation and at least, at its mildest, exploitation."[11] Since these are the very qualities that allow living things to flourish, asks Nietzsche, why are they considered evil? Or if we wish to call them evil, why should we not then recognize that just such evil is the foundation of all that is good? Or why not just go beyond good and evil? The question is not whether something is good or evil (or even true or false), but "to what extent it is life-promoting, life-preserving, species-preserving, perhaps even species-cultivating."[12]

And here we have the second difference with Darwin: Darwin was bent on explaining how the struggle to survive brought about higher, more complex traits and attributes in animals and especially in human beings. Nietzsche went beyond mere survival to flourishing, to fully expressing one's powers in the most magnificent way. Not mere survival of the fittest, but the will-to-power—that was the most important biological fact: "Physiologists should think before putting down the instinct of self-preservation as the cardinal instinct of an organic being. A living thing seeks above all to *discharge* its strength—life itself is *will to power*; self-preservation is only one of the indirect and most frequent *results*."[13]

We might sum up this difference by saying that in the survival of the fittest, Darwin focused on survival and Nietzsche focused on the fittest. Plankton merely survive; lions exude magnificent power. The real heart of evolution is not merely the desire to live but the will to power of the fittest, their inner drive to dominate, to spread out and consume all lesser beings. Aristocracy, then, is "incarnate will to power" which is not satisfied with mere life but "will strive to grow, spread, seize, become predominant—not from any morality or immorality but because it is living and because life simply is will to power."[14]

We come now to a third difference with Darwin. While both Darwin and Nietzsche considered different moralities to have arisen as after effects of the struggle to survive, Nietzsche divides them into

two essential kinds, the morality of the fit and the unfit, the aristocrat and the democrat, "*master morality* and *slave morality*."[15]

Master morality is natural morality, built upon the natural
ascendancy of the more fit over the less fit, the stronger over the
weaker, better over the worse. For the natural master, the natural
aristocrat, there is no opposition of good and evil; he divides things
between "'noble' and 'contemptible,'" master-like and slave-like.[16]
Whatever is strong and great is good, whatever is weak and trivial
is bad. In contrast, slave morality is the attempt by the weaker to
protect themselves from the stronger, to endure their sorry lot, and
to make themselves as comfortable as possible:

> Suppose the violated, oppressed, suffering, unfree, who are
> uncertain of themselves and weary, moralize: what will their
> moral valuations have in common?... The slave's eye is not favor-
> able to the virtues of the powerful: he is skeptical and suspicious,
> *subtly* suspicious, of all the "good" that is honored there [by the
> aristocrat]—he would like to persuade himself that even their
> happiness is not genuine. Conversely, [in slave morality] those
> qualities are brought out and flooded with light which serve to
> ease existence for those who suffer: here pity, the complaisant
> and obliging hand, the warm heart, patience, industry, humility,
> and friendliness are honored—for here these are the most useful
> qualities and almost the only means for enduring existence [for
> the slave]. Slave morality is essentially a morality of utility.[17]

Here we cannot help but recognize that the "virtues" of slave
morality bear a striking resemblance to virtues honored by Christianity. This also brings us, at last, to the core of Nietzsche's atheism. Nietzsche considered Christianity to be (at least in certain

respects) a species of slave morality, and hence a cause of the West's degradation. In focusing God's love on the weak, the least, the slaves, the poor, Christian charity has worked "to preserve all that was sick and that suffered—which means, in fact and in truth, to *worsen the European race.*"[18]

> Christianity has been the most calamitous kind of arrogance yet. Men, not high and hard enough to have any right to form *man* as artists; men, not strong and farsighted enough to *let* the foreground law of thousandfold failure and ruin prevail, though it cost them sublime self-conquest; men, not noble enough to see the abysmally different order of rank, chasm of rank, between man and man—*such* men have so far held sway over the fate of Europe, with their "equal before God," until finally a smaller, almost ridiculous type, a herd animal, something eager to please, sickly, and mediocre has been bred, the European of today.[19]

If we might put it this way, first Judaism[20] and then Christianity began to undermine natural aristocracy by asserting equality before God and elevating concern for the poor, the downtrodden, the slave, the sick, and the weak, and hence prepared the way for the modern passion for equality, democracy, and acceptance of the utilitarian belief that the goal of society is the elimination of suffering and the maximization of pleasure. But as we have seen, utilitarianism was essentially atheistic, commandeering a diluted form of Christian charity without the moral rigor and ultimate demands of a judging God, and directing all moral effort at maximizing the physical pleasure of the greatest number, thereby creating the "herd animal...the European of today."

Historically, then, Christianity in its original form was transformed into liberal Christianity, and finally into godless utilitarian liberalism. In this transformation, all the original asceticism, the absolute demands, the passionate desire to suffer with and for Christ, the difficult virtues, the awe before the divine, the self-abnegation, and the saintly heroic struggle were degraded through liberal Christianity and then through godless utilitarian liberalism into a kind of charity of softness that demanded nothing while it provided for every earthly comfort. This destruction of Christianity therefore brought about the utilitarian "green-pasture happiness of the herd, with security, lack of danger, comfort, and an easier life for everyone" wherein "the two songs and doctrines which they repeat most often are 'equality of rights' and 'sympathy for all that suffers'—and suffering itself they take for something that must be *abolished.*"[21] In this sense, Nietzsche the adamant atheist and self-proclaimed "AntiChrist" could lament the death of God: it has led to the ultimate "animalization of man into the dwarf animal of equal rights and claims."[22]

The cure for all this, trumpets Nietzsche, is a return to natural aristocracy. Slave morality calls everything that is noble, harsh, and demanding "evil." Natural aristocracy, like Darwinian nature itself, is pitiless and cruel in its demand for greatness and its contempt for the slave-like desire for mere physical pleasure and comfort. To keep Europe from its ultimate degeneration we must go beyond the slave distinction between good and evil and replace it with the aristocratic distinction between noble and contemptible, strong and weak.

This was not a merely philosophic project, as some scholars of Nietzsche like to claim. He was out to solve the "European problem" by "the cultivation of a new caste that will rule Europe."[23] To galvanize the dormant aristocratic element and revive Europe, a great danger needed to present itself, one that would awaken men from their utilitarian slumber and call forth the desire to fight and conquer:

> I mean such an increase in the menace of Russia [for example]
> that Europe would have to resolve to become menacing, too,
> namely, *to acquire one will* by means of a new caste that would
> rule Europe, a long, terrible will of its own that would be able to
> cast its goals millennia hence—so that the long-drawn-out com-
> edy of its many splinter states as well as its dynastic and demo-
> cratic splinter wills would come to an end. The time for petty
> politics is over: the very next century will bring the fight for the
> dominion of the earth—the *compulsion* to large-scale politics.[24]

One cannot help but hear the marching boots of the Third
Reich, an obvious inference that liberal academic propagandists of
Nietzsche vehemently deny. But it is not enough (as they would
have it) to find scattered pro-Jewish[25] and anti-German statements
in Nietzsche to clear him of such charges. It is possible that Nietzsche, had he lived three more decades, would not have approved
of how Hitler went beyond good and evil to solve the European
problem. Nevertheless, Nietzsche issued the call that Hitler, in his
own way, answered.

Nietzsche completed the modern rejection of God that began
with Machiavelli. He made clear to those who swallowed his words
what the real implications of godlessness were—a world without
good and evil, a world ruled by the will to power. Already in 1884
strange megalomaniacal utterances were finding their way into his
letters and books. In his letters he spoke of striking "a destructive
blow against Christianity," launching the "greatest decisive war in
history" where "we shall have convulsions on the earth such as
have never been," announcing that "the old god is abolished, and
that I myself will henceforth rule the world," and signing himself
"Nietzsche Caesar," "The Anti-Christian Friedrich Nietzsche," or
more tersely, "The Antichrist."[26] In 1885, amidst such revelries,

Nietzsche would begin *Beyond Good and Evil,* publishing it the following year. *Der AntiChrist* was written in 1888 but not published until 1894.

Nietzsche's complete dedication to drinking to the bitterest dregs the full depths of atheism ended in his own drop into the depths of insanity in January 1889, only four months after writing *Der AntiChrist.* The last decade of his life was spent in the darkest corners of madness, deteriorating in every way, at one stretch keeping everyone in the house awake repeating like a hideous drum, "I am dead because I am stupid...I am stupid because I am dead."[27]

In August 1900, Nietzsche was laid to rest next to his father, a pastor who had died when Friedrich was only four. But Nietzsche's fame and influence were just beginning, helping to take the century just then dawning far, far beyond good and evil. Even before his death, Nietzsche's thought was catching on. A kind of Nietzsche cult was building up slowly and surely, and after his death, this continued apace. We will examine Nietzsche's influence on his fellow Germans in our chapter on Hitler, but readers should be aware that there is more to evil than that displayed by the Nazis, as our next figure, the atheist Lenin, will make evident. Nietzsche, as the apostle of atheism, heralded the darkest century the world has ever known.

CHAPTER NINE

The State and Revolution
(1917)

> "*The proletariat needs state power, the centralized organization of force, the organization of violence, for the purpose of crushing the resistance of the exploiters. . . .*"
> Vladimir Ilyich Lenin (1870–1924)

THE FIRST THING TO SAY ABOUT LENIN IS THAT HIS REAL NAME WAS not Lenin, but Vladimir Ilyich Ulyanov. The name "Lenin" was just one of 160 or so aliases he used as a hunted revolutionary, chosen only because it was the one he happened to use for his first successful revolutionary work, *What Is to Be Done?*

The second is that the Ulyanovs were not oppressed Russian peasants but members of the upper class (and, interestingly enough, had relatively little Russian blood). Being part of the landed nobility, they benefited from the rule of the czars. Lenin was not a member of the proletariat. He was a privileged aristocrat who received the very best of educations and who never had to earn a living. Like Marx, he was far more interested in abstract theory than flesh-and-blood individuals, and so had very little contact with the working masses he was allegedly carrying to the communist promised land. That, perhaps, is why he had so little difficulty having them shot by the thousands when they balked at boarding the revolutionary express (or merely turned up late for work).

Third, Lenin was the man who, through his unifying vision and dominating personality, brought about the Bolsheviks' great October Russian Revolution of 1917, stamping the defining features on the most tyrannical government that has ever existed. While Lenin killed his millions, and Stalin killed his tens of millions, we should not be fooled into thinking, as the leftist hagiographers of Lenin would have it, that Stalin represented a deviation from the more lenient and humane Lenin. Lenin's brutality was less than his successor's only because he died fairly young. Stalin picked up precisely where Lenin left off and was successful in slaughtering his own countrymen in large part because of the intellectual and political system Lenin had established.

Lenin's *The State and Revolution* was written just before the Bolsheviks seized power from the more liberal revolutionaries who had brought an end to the rule of the czars about eight months previously. His book represents an amalgam of influences, direct and indirect, from Machiavelli, Hobbes, and Marx to the Westernizing efforts of Peter the Great and Catherine the Great in the eighteenth century and the violent pre-Marxian Russian revolutionaries. We shall treat each of these influences as we take a look at the text.

Let's begin with an overview of Lenin's argument. For Marx, and hence for Lenin, history is a relentless, driving conflict of classes that ends with a final revolution ushering in a communist utopia. We see in the very opening lines that the most obvious influence on Lenin's *The State and Revolution* is Marxism; Lenin declares that his "first task is to *restore* the true doctrine of Marx on the state."[1]

This might seem like a purely theoretical undertaking, but the restoration of the "true doctrine" meant to Lenin the vehement rejection of any political compromise. What stood in the way had to be ruthlessly and completely destroyed, both in speech and deed: "the liberation of the oppressed class is impossible, not only without violent revolution, *but also without the destruction* of the apparatus of state power."[2] Lenin seemed to savor the notion of violence. There could be no compromise with capitalism or capitalists. The bourgeoisie, the oppressive capitalist class, must be ferociously annihilated by the workers they oppressed, and a new revolutionary government built on the corpses. The revolutionary class is thereby given "the opportunity to crush, to smash to atoms, to wipe off the face of the earth the bourgeois, even the republican bourgeois, state machine, the standing army, the police and bureaucracy," and then "to substitute for all this a *more* democratic, but still a state machine in the shape of the armed masses of workers who become transformed into a universal people's militia."[3] To say it more simply, the revolutionaries must kill the capitalists, seize their property, and set up a "dictatorship of the proletariat."[4]

Lenin's characterization of the state as a machine is not mere metaphor. Marxism borrows Cartesian mechanism, squeezing the spirit out of the machine. The state is a machine because man is merely mechanical, a thing built accidentally by evolution, but which can be reforged purposely by revolutionary force. The dictatorship of the proletariat will wield the final hammer.

This proletarian dictatorship is democratic in this sense only. When the capitalists were in charge they ruled by the majority—the majority of the bourgeoisie, that is. When the proletariat smash the capitalistic form of democracy, they will replace it with the rule of the majority of the proletariat class. But here, majority rule will be absolute rule. The proletarian must iron out every capitalist wrinkle left in the social fabric. Hence, it will be a democratic dictatorship.

As noted already, the dictatorship of the proletariat is to be the last state. In Engels's words, which Lenin quotes approvingly, "The proletariat seizes the state power and transforms the means of production...into state property. But in doing this, it puts an end to itself as the proletariat, it puts an end to all class differences and class antagonisms, it puts an end also to the state as the state.... The state is not 'abolished,' *it withers away*."[5]

The state becomes absolute only to become obsolete. It withers away because everybody cheerfully rules on behalf of everybody else, and so nobody needs to rule over anybody. The coercive state—which for Marx and Lenin is the only kind of state—then disappears, leaving an entirely non-coercive society. In the words of Marx, this stateless "society [can] inscribe on its banners: from each according to his ability, to each according to his needs!"[6] Society exists without a state, no one owns anything because everyone owns everything, and all is well for the first time in human history.

G. K. Chesterton once said that communism eliminates the pickpocket by eliminating the pocket. That was far too generous. In Lenin's view, the man who owns the pants must be shot for having pockets, the pickpocket must be made the executioner, and all those watching the spectacle must be forced to make pocketless pants or else they too will be shot. Such is communism's brutal insanity. Under Lenin, somewhere between six to eight million people were slaughtered. Under Stalin, who inherited the "efficiently operating machinery for the mass destruction of political and social opponents," twenty to twenty-five million people were killed.[7] This nearly unimaginable butchery, perpetrated upon the very people it claimed to be benefiting, was not merely the result of Lenin's establishment of a dictatorship invested with the power to destroy all opposition. It was also caused by abolishing any qualms of conscience about using any means to achieve a merely political goal, a very Machiavellian idea indeed. (Lenin was a great admirer of Machiavelli.[8])

Lenin used three interlinked tools to abolish the idea of conscience. The first was atheism (also used by Machiavelli). Lenin was an atheist by the time he was sixteen, and as his more recent biographers make clear, his approach to politics was entirely amoral. A world without God meant one's hands were not tied by morality. Therefore any means were justified to achieve the desired political ends. The second tool followed upon this atheism. Lenin denied that there was a kingdom of heaven, and insisted instead that a communist utopia could be created on earth. The goal was painted as so wonderful—though in fact unachievable—and so progressive that anyone standing in its way deserved to be crushed.

The third tool was rooted in Marxism itself, especially in Lenin's interpretation of it. As viewed by the atheists Marx and Lenin, history has nothing to do with the unfolding of God's providence and the working out of man's free will. History inevitably marches, dialectical step by dialectical step, revolution by revolution, toward the utopian paradise of communism. Because this is an inevitable historical process, there can be no guilt about helping history swab the decks of all those who resist the inevitable. Indeed, sweeping brutality is meritorious. The faster and more thoroughly the opposition to historical progress toward utopia is swept away, the more quickly utopia can be reached.

With that overview, let's get a closer look at the arguments of *The State and Revolution*. As we've seen, Lenin was obsessed with purity of Marxist doctrine. Those who would allow any political reconciliation or introduce notions of peaceful reform rather than violent revolution must themselves be destroyed as enemies of revolutionary progress. Lenin's logic is simple and brutal. As history must go forward, there has to be a final revolution by which the rule of the capitalists is replaced by the rule of the workers. To bring about the desired communist utopia, every last scrap of capitalism must be destroyed by the proletarian dictators (or, more accurately, all capitalists must be treated as scraps, even while the proletariat commandeers their land, factories, and machinery). Capitalists must be killed as intransigent and irredeemable. Since capitalists are the only ones who could possibly oppose the glorious future envisioned by the proletarian dictators, all compromisers must therefore be capitalists. The simplicity of the logic is this: if you disagree with Lenin and the Bolsheviks, even if you are a Marxist, you must really be a capitalist. The brutality of the logic is even simpler: you must be destroyed as a more dangerous thing than an avowed capitalist.

Lenin therefore has nothing but venom in *The State and Revolution* for any Marxists or socialists who dare to disagree and suggest political compromise—Mensheviks, Kautskyites, petty bourgeois philistines and democrats, Socialist-Revolutionaries, the Kerensky government that overthrew the czar and held tentative power, social chauvinists and opportunists, and on and on. Lenin's book was largely a manifesto for purifying Marxism of every such non-Leninist.

When Lenin and the Bolsheviks finally seized power in the October Revolution, *The State and Revolution* became the officially sanctioned statement of the pure form of Marxism. This is an extremely important point. The future Soviet Union was the first Marxist state, the first down-to-earth practical incarnation of Marx's speculative theory. Lenin, in giving Marxism its first flesh and bones, defined Marxism for every Marxist state thereafter. In the words of Dmitri Volkogonov, "Lenin and Leninism became a state religion for atheists,"[9] and *The State and Revolution* was the official interpretive text clarifying why Marxism had to be Leninism.

Once the Bolsheviks under Lenin gained power, they were able to shoot down (literally) Marxist and socialist compromisers in debates. Lenin shaped the entire state apparatus, which was directed primarily at uprooting enemies of the people, including the people themselves.

To understand the full macabre nature of the Bolshevik state, we need to grasp that Lenin, following Marx and Engels, viewed the state as a purely negative thing—an idea that came ultimately from Hobbes. Hobbes declared, we recall, that our natural condition is pre-social and amoral. In the state of nature, we can do anything we like, even kill and eat other human beings. But this amoral condition is chaotic precisely because other human beings want to kill and eat us. Since we become caught in a state of war, we all decide to give up our right to do anything we please and give some individual absolute power over all of us. This sovereign of civil society is the state, since his will, however arbitrary, is law. Hence Hobbes portrayed the state as entirely negative: born out of chaos, it exists only to suppress chaos.

Marx, Engels, and Lenin adopted this idea, but rather than focusing on individuals in the state of nature, they focused on classes. Thus the "state is the product and the manifestation of the *irreconcilability* of class antagonisms."[10] That is why the state does not and cannot act as "an organ for the *conciliation* of classes."[11] If there could be reconciliation, Lenin thunders, there wouldn't be a need for the state to begin with. The state is by definition irredeemably oppressive. Those given power in the state will always rule for themselves and their own class at the expense of another class. Consequently, the state is always "an organ of class *rule*, the organ for the *oppression* of one class by another" because it is "the product of irreconcilable class antagonisms."[12]

As the Marxist historical dialectic has it, oppressors never give up power and never compromise; therefore, they can be crushed only by revolution of the oppressed. Every state must then yield to violent revolution. Any attempt at political compromise by those in power is merely a way for them to hold on to power. Any suggestion by fellow revolutionaries that there can be compromise is a sign of treason.

Why, we might ask, would we expect the dictatorship of the proletariat to be any different? Why should the workers' state be any different from any previous state? Won't they become enamored with their power and privilege? Won't they also become just one more collective oppressor of those they rule?

The historical, factual answer is "yes." The Soviet house that Lenin built became an absolute dictatorship of the few, whose ruthless rule was aimed at a target near and dear to them—their own power and privilege.

The entirely fictional, ideological answer—the one given by Marx, Engels, and Lenin—is "no." The proletarian state, they insist, will wither away. All oppression by the dictatorship of the proletariat will exist solely to end all capitalist oppression.

The greatest trick of Bolshevism, one that would make even Machiavelli jealous, was to make the miserable masses under Soviet rule imagine that their misery was for their own good—in fact, the greatest possible good imaginable for the entire world, a utopian reign of peace and plenty in a global stateless society without struggle or coercion. Given this vision, they would cheerfully and willingly endure the most oppressive government in history for the sake of removing governmental oppression once and for all. (Or be shot.)

The obvious problem is that oppression is a monster that feeds upon itself, rather than leading to something better. Despite the rosy picture, the Bolshevik mindset—Lenin's own mindset—was bent upon seeing all dissent, even the dissent of common sense, as leftover capitalist opposition against which all the powers of the militarized revolutionary state should be unleashed for the sake of "crushing the inevitable and desperate resistance of the bourgeoisie."[13]

But ripping up the pestiferous bourgeois weeds was by no means the only Bolshevik passion. Like Peter the Great and Catherine the Great, Lenin believed passionately that largely agrarian Russia had to be Westernized, and to him that meant industrialized. This was a matter of Marxist purity. According to the theory, communism had to follow upon capitalist industrialism; it couldn't be built on an agrarian base. Therefore, the proletariat dictators had to rush the population forward into the industrial age, doing in months what had taken other nations many decades, even centuries. In Leninist lingo, this was called "organizing *all* the toiling and exploited masses for the new economic order."[14] As the toiling and exploited masses were now free of their capitalist oppressors, they would gladly work for little or nothing for the state as equal comrades. (Or be shot.)

Lenin was big on terror as a form of discipline. He felt a kinship with the Russian agrarian socialists, the *narodniki*, who advocated the use of violence and terror to bring down imperial rule. While he rejected their adherence to the old Russian peasant ideal (opting instead for a Marxist industrialized Russia), he found their use of terror inspiring, before and especially after the revolution. For example, once in power, the communists had to prove the superiority of their system over capitalism, which meant that communist laborers had to produce more than capitalist laborers. But communist laborers often had leftover bourgeois values, like wanting to take a day off occasionally, such as on the festival of St. Nicholas, the patron saint of Russia. That was a double affront to the atheist Lenin. "It's stupid to be reconciled to the 'Nikola' festival. We must get all the Chekas [the secret police thugs] up on their feet and shoot people who don't turn up for work because of the 'Nikola' festival." He believed the same should be done on Christmas and New Year's Day celebrations.[15]

The hardness of Lenin's heart was the direct result of his belief that full industrialization, achieved by any means, was the last necessary step before the state could wither away. Lenin had no anxiety at all, then, about pushing workers to achieve industrial quotas, even if it meant driving a good number into an early grave or to Siberia. As he said, "*We ourselves*, the workers, will organize large-scale production" and "we shall establish strict, iron discipline supported by the state power of the armed workers."[16] Lenin never worked a day in his life, at least as a proletarian. He was one of the "vanguard," the Marxist theoreticians. So the comradely "we" was entirely fictional, as was the very notion that the workers really would rule in the proletariat dictatorship; that role was reserved for the vanguards.[17] The bit about the iron discipline as meted out by "armed" comrades was, however, entirely factual. As we've noted, once in power, the Bolsheviks (most of whom were revolutionary academics like Lenin) decided that missing work or merely showing up late was cause for being shot or being given a ticket to Siberia. Such was the life of the happy "organized" proletariat.

We should mention that while Lenin liked peasant-terrorists, he had an especial disdain for the peasantry itself (who made up about 85 percent of the population). They represented the backward status of Russia as compared to the more industrialized nations of Europe. The peasants were a class that should long ago have been replaced by an industrial working class—such was the demand of Marxist historical dialectic. And as they were historical holdovers,

Lenin felt no anxiety about sacrificing them to progress. Even as a young man, when he heard about mass starvation among the peasants, his stone-hearted reaction was purely Marxist: don't interfere, let them starve. Because starvation must be caused by capitalism, mass starvation was good. It showed that history was moving forward, through conflict, toward the final revolution of the proletariat.[18]

The State and Revolution was the blueprint for Bolshevik blackness, written on the darkening eve of the revolution. It was an apology for absolute power that gave ambiguous indications of its future absolute corruption. For example:

> The proletariat needs state power, the centralized organization of force, the organization of violence, for the purpose of crushing the resistance of the exploiters and for the purpose of *leading* the great mass of the population—the peasantry, the petty bourgeoisie, the semi-proletarians—in the work of organizing socialist economy.[19]

If you read this quickly, it sounds like the organization of violence is directed only against crushing the resistance of the capitalist exploiters, and once crushed, the violent aspects of the organization could be left behind. But Lenin meant that the organization of violence will continue to be necessary "for the purpose of *leading* the great mass of the population—the peasantry, the petty bourgeoisie, the semi-proletarians—in the work of organizing socialist economy." Just to allay fears, Lenin promised that "it will entail far less bloodshed than the suppression of the risings of slaves, serfs or wage-laborers" under capitalism, therefore "it will cost mankind far less."[20]

Was Lenin lying? I suspect not. He really did believe that the extermination of opposition would be a relatively bloodless affair.

After all, capitalists are in the minority; oppressed workers and peasants are in the majority. How long can it take to get rid of the minority?

In truth, it is Lenin's very naïveté that magnifies his later brutality. He just couldn't believe that the opposition to his utopian dreams could be so real and widespread. How could so many people dare to stand against his perfectly elucidated vision of Marx? The fury at being contradicted in theory fed his rage in destroying all contradictions in practice. So it was that the communist state apparatus came to be defined by the politicization of rage. As we've mentioned, the Soviet-style Marxist government became the pattern for, and patron of, the other equally barbarous communist governments that crushed so many more millions of lives (at least another 40 million, if not double that; *The Black Book of Communism* estimates 100 million) in Eastern Europe, North Korea, Vietnam, China, Cambodia, and Cuba. Such is the legacy of the state as defined by Lenin's *The State and Revolution.*

CHAPTER TEN

The Pivot of Civilization (1922)

> *"[E]ach feeble-minded person is a potential source of endless progeny of defect; we prefer the policy of immediate sterilization, [so] that parenthood is absolutely prohibited to the feeble-minded. . . . "*
>
> Margaret Sanger (1879–1966)

IF YOU WOULD LIKE TO PURCHASE YOUR OWN COPY OF MARGARET Sanger's book *The Pivot of Civilization*, you will not find a copy for sale on the Planned Parenthood Web site. That is rather strange, given that Sanger is the foundress of Planned Parenthood and this is one of her most famous books. The Web site does, of course, acknowledge Sanger's authorship, but only by way of admitting that "Sanger...entertained some popular ideas of her own time that are out of keeping with our thinking today." And, moreover, "Planned Parenthood Federation of America finds these views," or at least some of her views, "objectionable and outmoded."

What were these views so "out of keeping with our thinking today"? Sanger was a red-hot eugenicist, publishing her great eugenic work, *The Pivot of Civilization*, three years before Adolf Hitler wrote his own eugenic masterpiece, *Mein Kampf.* You see the problem. As we've noted, eugenics got a bad name after the Nazis, but the gritty truth is that in championing eugenics Margaret Sanger did not just entertain "some popular ideas of her own time." She was one of the great leaders of the international eugenics movement, and the connections between the eugenic aspirations of pre–World War II Americans and Germans is a matter of hard facts.[1] Even more revealing, Sanger didn't peddle birth control and also espouse eugenic views, as if these were two unrelated passions. Eugenics was at the very heart of her reasons for pushing birth control.

One can see why Planned Parenthood would engage in what amounts to the soft censorship of Sanger's book. Fortunately, *The Pivot of Civilization* is now available from a number of publishers and can also be found online, so readers may judge for themselves how entertaining her "popular ideas" were. I, for one, am happy that it has escaped censorship.

So, down to the dirty business of reading a very bad book. *The Pivot of Civilization* addresses "the greatest present menace to . . . civilization": the "lack of balance between the birth-rate of the 'unfit' and the 'fit,'" a menace precisely because of the "fertility of the feeble-minded, the mentally defective, [and] the poverty-stricken." Sanger believed that "the most urgent problem of to-day is how to limit and discourage the over-fertility of the mentally and physically defective." This scourge calls for hard-knuckled action, and indeed "possibly drastic and Spartan methods may be forced upon American society if it continues complacently to encourage the chance and chaotic breeding that has resulted from our stupid, cruel sentimentalism."[2]

While "feeble-mindedness" is not the only smudge Sanger hoped to cleanse from the population, her concern with it bordered on an obsession. Just to be clear, at that time the term "feeble-minded" indicated a whole range of substandard intelligence. Psychologists had ranked relative intelligence according to mental age; the first Intelligence Quotient (IQ) was calculated according to this formula:

IQ = mental age ÷ chronological age x 100

Obviously, if your mental age matched your chronological age, then you were a "100." But the more your mental age lagged behind your chronological age, the more "feeble-minded" you could be considered. According to this scale, an "idiot" had an IQ of 0–25, an "imbecile," 26–50, and a "moron," 51–70. Sanger's book is one long rant against the existence—and worse, the breeding—of the "feeble-minded" in general, and the "moron," "imbecile," and "idiot" in particular, those "who never should have been born at all."[3] Against these menaces, Sanger proposes "Birth Control" as the "very pivot of civilization," meaning that the future of civilization depended upon birth control to severely reduce—if not eliminate—feeble-mindedness from the human population. Birth control was, in her mind, the "greatest and most truly eugenic method," and she promised that "its adoption as part of the program of Eugenics would immediately give a concrete and realistic power to that science. As a matter of fact," Sanger assures the reader, "Birth Control has been accepted by the most clear thinking and far seeing of the Eugenicists themselves as the most constructive and necessary of the means to racial health."[4]

Let us look more deeply into this great problem of feeble-mindedness, which, if we take Sanger's alarums seriously, was spreading like an insidious plague, threatening the future of the human race. The "great problem of the feeble-minded . . . as the best authorities agreed, [is] to prevent the birth of those who would transmit imbecility to their descendants." Here's the rub: "Feeble-mindedness . . . is invariably associated with an abnormally high rate of fertility," i.e., stupid people are breeding like rabbits, a lot faster than the bright folk. And the problem wasn't just that the unfit were outbreeding the fit. It was that feeble-mindedness was the "fertile parent of degeneracy, crime, and pauperism." In fact, "Modern studies indicate that insanity, epilepsy, criminality, prostitution, pauperism, and mental defect, are all organically bound up together and that the least intelligent and the thoroughly degenerate classes in every community are the most prolific. Feeble-mindedness in one generation becomes pauperism or insanity in the next."[5]

This, by the way, was a very Darwinian thing to say, as we recall from our chapter on Darwin's *Descent of Man.* As morality is one more evolved trait, then it is clear that it can become an inherited characteristic. At the heart of morality, in Darwin's view, was sympathy. If someone doesn't happen to inherit the sympathy trait, "then he is essentially a bad man."[6] Good breeding, therefore, makes good morality: "There is not the least inherent improbability, as it seems to me, in virtuous tendencies being more or less strongly inherited.... If bad tendencies are transmitted, it is probable that good ones are likewise transmitted. Excepting through the principle of the transmission of moral tendencies, we cannot understand the differences believed to exist in this respect between the various *races* of mankind."[7] The problem, Darwin bemoaned, was that "the very poor and reckless, who are often degraded by vice, almost invariable marry early, whilst the careful and frugal, who are generally otherwise virtuous, marry late in life, so that they may be able to support themselves and their children in comfort." The dread result is that those who marry early "produce many more children." The inevitable outcome: "the reckless, degraded, and often vicious members of society, tend to increase at a quicker rate than the provident and generally virtuous members." We all know what this means. Darwin quotes W. R. Greg with great approval:

The careless, squalid, unaspiring Irishman multiplies like rabbits: the frugal, foreseeing, self-respecting Scot, stern in his morality, spiritual in his faith, sagacious and disciplined in his intelligence, passes his best years in struggle and in celibacy, marries late, and leaves few behind him. Given a land originally peopled by a thousand Saxons and a thousand Celts—and in a dozen generations five-sixths of the population would be Celts, but five-sixths of the property, of the power, of the intellect, would belong to the one-sixth of Saxons that remained. In the eternal "struggle for existence," it would be the inferior and *less* favoured race that had prevailed—and prevailed by virtue not of its good qualities but of its faults.[8]

There you have it. A cold shudder indeed. Think of it, the future landscape with nothing but unaspiring Irishmen multiplying off into the horizon, while the Great Scot sits sternly on his island of morality, its shores ever receding under the encroaching squalid tide.

Speaking of feeble-mindedness, Darwin viewed mental retardation as a sign of his theory's truth: it represented an atavistic eruption, a sudden instance of our ape ancestors peeking through to remind us of our humble origins. "The simple brain of a microcephalous idiot, in as far as it resembles that of an ape, may in this sense be said to offer a case of reversion."[9] So, the small-brained were evolutionary backsliders. And Darwin noted, in this regard, that the "skull in Europeans is 92.3 cubic inches," whereas those of the racial lowbrows, the "Asiatics" and "Australians," were only 87.1 and 81.9 cubic inches respectively. Of course, in "Americans" the "mean internal capacity of the skull" was only 87.5.[10]

Sanger was obviously a good Darwinian, putting all this together in a nice eugenic package. Instead of focusing on race, however, she (both following and leading other eugenicists of her day) emphasized relative intelligence. That makes the problem of immorality, of evil, very simple. Evil is not caused by sin. There is no such thing as an evil genius. The original sin that causes all our ills, passed from generation to overabundant generation, is low IQ. In order to fix once and for all the nasty ills that have beset every society—but especially societies that allow the feebleminded to breed indiscriminately—we need only to stop the stupid from breeding.

But lest she be misunderstood, Sanger's fundamental problem with feeblemindedness was not that those affected are the cause of every possible evil and crime. The "menace of feeble-mindedness to the race" is that they exist at all. She admits the existence of the "so-called 'good feeble-minded,'" who could be "fostered in a 'suitable environment,'" and so be made into a "docile, tractable, and peaceable element of the community." But she will brook no starry-eyed sentimentalism:

> In such a reckless and thoughtless differentiation between the "bad" and the "good" feeble-minded, we find new evidence of the conventional middle-class bias that also finds expression among some of the eugenicists. We do not object to feeble-mindedness simply because it leads to immorality and criminality; nor can we approve of it when it expresses itself in docility, submissiveness and obedience. We object because both are burdens and dangers to the intelligence of the community. As a matter of fact, there is sufficient evidence to lead us to believe that the so-called "borderline cases" are a greater menace than the out-and-out "defective delinquents" who can be supervised, controlled and prevented from procreating their kind. The advent of the Binet-Simon [IQ test] and similar psychological tests indicates that the mental defective who is glib and plausible, bright looking and

attractive, but with a mental vision of seven, eight or nine years, may not merely lower the whole level of intelligence in a school or in a society, but may be encouraged by church and state to increase and multiply until he dominates and gives the prevailing "color"—culturally speaking—to an entire community.[11]

Some might underplay the "menace of the moron...because of their alleged small numerical proportion to the rest of the population," but:

> The actual dangers can only be fully realized when we have acquired definite information concerning the financial and cultural cost of these classes to the community, when we become fully cognizant of the burden of the imbecile upon the whole human race; when we see the funds that should be available for human development, for scientific, artistic and philosophic research, being diverted annually, by hundreds of millions of dollars, to the care and segregation of men, women, and children who never should have been born.[12]

However, Sanger realizes "the dangers of interfering with personal liberty.... Nor do we believe that the community could or should send to the lethal chamber the defective progeny resulting from irresponsible and unintelligent breeding."[13] (Recall, this was written about a decade before the Nazi extermination program began.) But, that having been said:

> The emergency problem of segregation and sterilization must be faced immediately. Every feeble-minded girl or woman of the hereditary type, especially of the moron class, should be segregated during the reproductive period. Otherwise, she is almost

certain to bear imbecile children, who in turn are just as certain to breed other defectives. The male defectives are no less dangerous. Segregation carried out for one or two generations would give us only partial control of the problem. Moreover, when we realize that each feeble-minded person is a potential source of endless progeny of defect, we prefer the policy of immediate sterilization, of making sure that parenthood is absolutely prohibited to the feeble-minded.[14]

Well, one might wonder, just how many feeble-minded are there out there? Sanger is not clear. Taking the results of an Oregon study, she pegs it at about 10 percent.[15] Yet it is difficult to know how wide Sanger wished to cast her eugenic net because, along with the slippery designation of feeble-mindedness, she believed birth control was necessary to eliminate all mental and physical defects. These could number quite a few, because "authorities tell us that 75 per cent. of the school-children are defective." She notes that in the military draft of 1917, 38 percent of the men "were rejected because of physical ill-health and defects,"[16] and that in another "psychological examination of the drafted men . . . nearly half—47.3 per cent.— of the population had the mentality of twelve-year-old children or less—in other words . . . they were morons." She then quotes one Professor Conklin, who extrapolated from the draftees as "a fair sample of the entire population of approximately 100,000,000," that "45,000,000 or nearly one-half the entire population, will never develop mental capacity beyond the stage represented by a normal twelve-year-old child."[17] Imagine that. Every other person you meet on the street is a moron, fit for forced sterilization!

However many there are, and however difficult it would be to detect them, Sanger felt one thing for certain. The "debauch of sentimentalism," the "cruelty of charity" that only makes the problem worse must be avoided. Also taboo was the Christian notion of charity based on the sanctity of human life, which sees each human being as made in the image of God. Such charity "encourages the healthier and more normal sections of the world to shoulder the burden of unthinking and indiscriminate fecundity of others; which brings with it, as I think the reader must agree, a dead weight of human waste. Instead of decreasing and aiming to eliminate the stocks that are most detrimental to the future of the race and the world, it tends to render them to a menacing degree dominant."[18]

One need only think of those squalid, unaspiring Irish Catholics mentioned by W. R. Greg. Sanger was well aware of the Irish Catholic problem because her mother had been one and the Catholic Church was her most ardent opponent. (She herself was an atheist, guided in part by her radical father.) She reminded her readers that in America, the "dead weight of human waste" votes:

> The danger of recruiting our numbers from the most "fertile stocks" is further emphasized when we recall that in a democracy like that of the United States every man and woman is permitted a vote in the government, and that it is the representatives of this grade of intelligence who may destroy our liberties, and who may thus be the most far-reaching peril to the future of civilization.... Equality of political power has thus been bestowed upon the lowest elements of our population. We must not be surprised, therefore, at the spectacle of political scandal and graft, of the notorious and universally ridiculed low level of intelligence and flagrant stupidity exhibited by our legislative bodies. The Congressional Record mirrors our political imbecility.[19]

Imagine how C-SPAN would have stoked the righteous fires of Sanger's indignation. "The 'warm heart' needs the balance of the cool head."[20] Something must be done to close the "ever-widening margin of biological waste."[21]

If you've ever wondered at the religious-like fervor of the sexual education clique, and their scornful avoidance of democratic modes of implementation, you need only read Sanger. Same thing if you've ever wondered at the similar religious fervor of the sexual education clique at the United Nations: "Unless sexual science is incorporated as an integral part of world-statesmanship and the pivotal importance of Birth Control is recognized in any program of reconstruction, all efforts to create a new world and a new civilization are foredoomed to failure."[22]

Yet you will not fully understand the *religious* nature of the fervor until you catch sight of the absolutely bizarre spiritualization of sexuality advocated by Sanger. You see, sex isn't just for making babies. Quoting her sexual guru Havelock Ellis, sex is "the function by which all the finer activities of the organism, physical and psychic, may be developed and satisfied."[23] In fact, as Sanger elaborates, "Birth Control is an ethical necessity for humanity to-day because it places in our hands a new instrument of self-expression and self-realization."[24]

Skeptical? You must not be aware, as was Sanger, that the latest psychologists have affirmed that we have "inner energies, the greatest and most imperative of which are Sex and Hunger." Hunger creates "the struggle for existence" so profitable to evolutionary progress; it has "spurred men to the discovery and invention of methods and ways of avoiding starvation"; it has "developed primitive barter into our contemporary Wall Streets"; it has "developed thrift and economy" in conquering "King Hunger." Birth control also helps to subdue King Hunger by eliminating excess mouths to feed.[25]

But what about this other "inner energy"? Sanger views sex as another essentially creative force, "no less ceaseless in its dynamic energy."[26] The problem, she argues, is that this other energy remains largely untapped because it is only used for procreation (mostly of idiots). We need to release sexual energy itself, both from its baleful procreative result and from the moral taboos:

> The moment civilization is wise enough to remove the constraints and prohibitions which now hinder the release of inner energies, most of the larger evils of society will perish of inanition and malnutrition. Remove the moral taboos that now bind the human body and spirit, free the individual from the slavery of tradition, remove the chains of fear from men and women, above all answer their unceasing cries for knowledge that would make possible self-direction and salvation, and in so doing, you best serve the interests of society at large.[27]

Now you might wonder how chucking moral prohibitions and giving free reign to sexual desire would serve the interests of society. Please bear with me, because we are about to enter an extended exhibit in the Pseudo-Science Hall of Fame. We have in our bodies "ductless glands," which exude "secretions," and eminent scientists assure us that "the genesis and exercise of the higher faculties of men are conditioned by the purely chemical action of the product of these secretions." When we use these glands—especially the "reproductive glands"—the "internal secretions or endocrines pass directly into the blood stream, and exercise a dominating power over health and personality," not just in our body but in our "mental and psychic development as well."[28] So the more you use your glands, the greater your mental and psychic development. "Science" therefore "illuminates the whole problem of genius":

> Hidden in the common stuff of humanity lies buried this power of self-expression. Modern science is teaching us that genius is not some mysterious gift of the gods, some treasure conferred upon individuals chosen by chance.... Rather is it [i.e., genius] due to the removal of physiological and psychological inhibitions and constraints which makes possible the release and the channeling of the primordial inner energies of man into full and divine expression. The removal of these inhibitions, so scientists assure us, makes possible more rapid and profound perceptions,—so rapid indeed that they seem to the ordinary human being, practically instantaneous, or intuitive. The qualities of genius are not therefore, qualities lacking in the common reservoir of humanity, but rather the unimpeded release and direction of powers latent in all of us.[29]

Birth control not only keeps the dead weight of human waste from propagating, but for the lucky rest of us it allows an astounding increase in IQ. No wonder the future looks so rosy. "Let us look forward to this great release of creative and constructive energy," wherein "the great adventures in the enchanted realm of the arts and sciences may no longer be the privilege of a gifted few, but the rightful heritage of a race of genius."[30] How to bring about these great adventures? "The abolition of the shame and fear of sex.... Through sex, mankind may attain the great spiritual illumination which will transform the world, which will light up the only path to an earthly paradise. So must we necessarily and inevitably conceive of sex-expression."[31] We realize, by the time we get to Sanger's finale, that sex has become her god, her idol, her religion:

> Interest in the vague sentimental fantasies of extra-mundane existence, in pathological or hysterical flights from the realities of earthliness, will have through atrophy disappeared, for in that dawn men and women will have come to the realization, already suggested, that here close at hand is our paradise, our everlasting abode, our Heaven and our eternity. Not by leaving it and our essential humanity behind us, nor by sighing to be anything but what we are, shall we ever become ennobled or immortal. Not for woman only, but for all of humanity is this the field where we must seek the secret of eternal life.[32]

So ends Sanger's eugenic masterpiece. In assessing it, we must keep in mind the fundamental influence of Darwinism. "Eugenics," Sanger explained, "aims to seek out the root of our trouble, to study humanity as a kinetic, dynamic, evolutionary organism, shifting and changing with the successive generations, rising and falling, cleansing itself of inherent defects, or under adverse and dysgenic influences, sinking into degeneration and deterioration."[33] All Sanger's pseudo-science about genius-creating sexual glands aside, her desire to create a master race of geniuses, shorn of the dead weight of human waste, can only remind us of the equally despicable ruminations of Adolf Hitler (which we'll visit next). Sanger's book was part of a wide, pre–World War II international eugenic movement that united eugenic advocates in America, England, and Germany. While Sanger may not have directly influenced Hitler, it is undeniable that they drank from the same fetid intellectual pool.

But what, we should ask, is really wrong with eugenics? Granted that Hitler may have given it a momentarily bad name, yet we now seem to be hurtling full-throttle into a eugenic future: the elimination of the malformed or otherwise unfit through fetal screening; the manipulation of the genetic lottery through baby-designer technologies; the enhancement of our physique and our intelligence through genetic therapy. There seems no end to the eugenic possibilities that technology could provide. Should we be morally easy or morally queasy?

If we think back over Darwin and Sanger, especially in the context of the general modern intellectual milieu we've been sketching, we can begin to see the darkness behind the promising eugenic future. In falling more fully into the embrace of eugenicism, human imperfections would become increasingly held in contempt—a path that leads inevitably to barbarism. Just as Lenin beheld a frictionless communist utopia on the horizon and this vision of paradise fueled his savagery in removing everything in its way, so also the eugenicist will be animated by a vision of physical and mental perfection that will justify the destruction of any imperfections that blot his view. Those who stand in the way of eugenic utopia—whether it be on moral grounds or because they themselves have some alleged imperfection—will be considered enemies of human happiness and reminders of human misery. Imperfections themselves will become moral offenses: "How can you go ahead and have this child knowing it almost certainly is mentally retarded?" will slide into "You should have known there was a chance she would have red hair." The end result will be a promethean insistence on getting exactly what we want, and a seething discontent that insists on destroying anything less—a kind of monstrous cross between a spoiled child and a pitiless grim reaper.

Furthermore, if any problem seems eugenically fixable, then every problem will soon seem eugenically curable. We need not look any further than Sanger to see how sordid this could become. If crime, pauperism, alcoholism, and general feeble-mindedness (however defined) are *thought to be* the result of genetic imperfections, then the eugenist will want to get rid of those genes by getting rid of the gene carriers. All that it takes to construct a devouring eugenic juggernaut is the suspicion that there is some connection between particular genes and particular imperfections. In Sanger's deranged mind, a low or even moderate IQ was linked inextricably to nearly every social ill. It doesn't matter that she was wrong, what matters is if enough other people think she's right, and pseudo-science becomes well-funded public policy.

Another baneful result lurks in the shadows. One of the effects of becoming a utilitarian-based society, one that promotes pleasure as the highest good and pain as the highest evil, is an almost pathological softness in the face of any adversity. This pathology will yield all kinds of bizarre eugenic results, a prophecy that we can base firmly on the lunacy that already gallops regularly through the public square. The saying "Boys will be boys," has been replaced by the prescription, "Boys will need Ritalin." If parents and teachers now care so much for peace and so little for the natural good of boys that they have no moral qualms about doping them into near-somnolence, what will they say to the genomic genies who promise them kindler, gentler designer males?

We should also remember that eugenics is more than genetics; it includes the elimination of the unfit as well. We live in a society that has long ago slipped from allowing early abortion in "extreme" cases to abortion at any time for the most trivial of reasons, including eugenics. We are now sliding into infanticide for "extreme" cases, which, running in the same predictable ruts, will end in infanticide for even the most trivial reasons. If parents are obsessed with getting exactly the child they ordered, and believe in their Hobbesian souls that they have a *right* to it, then they will be proportionately incensed at getting less than they imagined and will claim a right to kill undesirables. There is already a eugenic industry set up that uses living organs and tissues from babies in the womb. There could easily be an industry that harvests organs from babies born for that purpose or that parents decided they don't want after all. One can imagine parents agreeing to infanticide, knowing that their unwanted offspring will be recycled for the eugenic enhancement of others.

Euthanasia, the killing on the other end of life, displays another face of eugenics. Here, too, we will quickly move from voluntary euthanasia of the incurably ill to involuntary euthanasia of the old and burdensome. Parents who have cared so little for their children that they cast them into daycare at six weeks and doped them with Ritalin and video games so they would not be bothered, will certainly have no compunction about eliminating their own parents when they too become bothersome. Even more likely, as aging parents require nursing care that eats up the inheritance, children will look at any illness as an excuse for extermination. Their rationalization will be quite simple and quite eugenic: any step down from a good life is a bad life, and there's only one way to go when you're old; just as we owe it to future generations to remove eugenically all that is less than perfect, the passing generation owes to the present generation the removal of its own imperfections.

And so, we should not envision our eugenic future according to the science fiction stories of perfect men and women systematically eliminating all that is imperfect. That would be bad enough, but what will actually occur—what is actually occurring—is far more miserable. What we are is what we will be, but even more so: an overweight, sickly society, obsessed with health and perfection but so addicted to pleasure and ease that the simplest exertions and smallest deprivations are excruciating; a people addicted to junk food, junk entertainment, and junk medicine who will grasp at any bottle of eugenic snake oil offered by conniving entrepreneurs more than willing to spin gullibility and desperation into mountains of cash. Our women will become just like those I mentioned from the Ukraine in the chapter on Machiavelli who gladly pay out thousands of dollars for freshly harvested baby parts in the vain hope of staving off the ravages of their own inevitable aging. Do not be surprised when you hear reports that Viagra has been superceded by treatments derived from rejuvenating "tissue" supplied by the same abortion clinics. That is the real future of Sanger's eugenic paradise.

CHAPTER ELEVEN

Mein Kampf
(1925)

*"On this planet of ours human culture and civilization
are indissolubly bound up with the presence of the Aryan.
If he should be exterminated or subjugated, then the dark
shroud of a new barbarian era would enfold the earth. . . . "*

Adolf Hitler (1889–1945)

MANY PEOPLE HAVE READ BOOKS ABOUT ADOLF HITLER, BUT ALL
too few have read Hitler's own book, *Mein Kampf* (*My Struggle*), a
book written prior to his coming to power while he was in jail for
instigating revolution. The danger of only reading about Hitler is
that one can easily get an entirely distorted view of him as an evil
madman rather than an evil genius. A madman is driven by mania
for a very particular idea; a genius is driven by a grand vision, a
malignant worldview. This distinction is essential for understanding the apex of Hitler's evil: his apparent mania for exterminating
the Jews. We might easily think that Hitler's genocidal ambitions
were rooted entirely in his virulent anti-Semitism. But *Mein Kampf*
helps to reveal that they were merely one malevolent effect of a far
deeper, more profound and pervasive evil, a *Weltanshauung* that
should by now look quite familiar to readers of this book. Hitler's

evil spirit was, in important respects, a specter of the most malignant tendencies of his time, of the *Zeitgeist*, the unholy spirit of the age that brooded over the chaos of Weimar Germany.

"It is a pretty barbarous business—one would not wish to go into details—and there are not many Jews left I should think. One could assume that about 60 percent of them have been liquidated and about 40 percent taken for forced labor.... One simply cannot be sentimental about these things.... The Führer is the moving spirit of this radical solution both in word and deed." So wrote Dr. Paul Joseph Goebbels in his diary entry of March 27, 1942. Goebbels was the Reich Minister for Popular Enlightenment and Propaganda, a man who had earned his Ph.D. in literature from Heidelberg University and whose intellectual development had been greatly influenced by Friedrich Nietzsche. "I expect you to do superhuman acts of inhumanity," Heinrich Himmler, commander of the dreaded Schutzstaffel (SS), told the Einsatzgruppen charged with removing the Jews from Poland. "But it is the Führer's will."[1]

Inhumanity was not so easily bought. Himmler learned that SS members were having nervous breakdowns and drinking heavily. Dutiful as he was, he decided to witness an atrocity for himself, ordering a particular Einsatzgruppe to shoot one hundred prisoners. And he himself was undone, watching two women writhing on the ground who had only been wounded in the first volley of bullets. "Don't torture those women!" Himmler ordered. "Get on with it, shoot quickly!" Afterward, he brought the men around him for a pep talk, assuring them that, as they were good Germans, they shouldn't enjoy this task, but as soldiers they should do their duty, knowing that he and Hitler bore the ultimate responsibility. Their consciences should rest at ease.[2] And so the corpses piled ever higher.

The Nazi regime murdered not only six million Jews but millions of other "undesirables": enemies of the Reich, from Slavs,

Gypsies, and prisoners of war, to the handicapped, retarded, and even mildly "unfit." The Aktion T4 program, the Nazi eugenic plan-in-action, resulted in the state-ordered execution of around 200,000 people who were disabled, retarded, juvenile delinquents, mixed-race children, or even plagued with significant adolescent acne.[3]

Given the epic scale of their inhumanity, we need to remember that the Nazi regime did not purport to do evil. It claimed to be scientific and progressive, to do what hard reason demanded for the ultimate benefit of the human race. The superhuman acts of inhumanity were carried out for the sake of humanity. Shouldn't we be concerned about the overall health of the race? Why shouldn't that be the highest good? Why shouldn't we ruthlessly root out the unfit who are a burden to themselves and others? Isn't it a good thing to seek medical advances, ways to save humanity from suffering?

Hard reason, but without the sympathy. One cannot help but be reminded of Darwin's *Descent of Man.* "National Socialism is nothing but applied biology," said the deputy Party leader of the Nazis, Rudolf Hess.[4] Repeating the Machiavellian and Nietzschean antagonism to religion, such applied biology clashed with charity: the ruthless application of Darwinian biological principles—the elimination of the unfit and the enhancement of the fit by all means—demanded an explicit rejection of Christianity. The Nazis were all for health, and Himmler championed the Greek physician Hippocrates as the paradigm of Nazi medicine. But, as psychiatrist Robert Lifton notes:

> There was one area in which the Nazis did insist upon a clear break with medical tradition [beginning with Hippocrates]. They mounted a consistent attack upon what they viewed as exaggerated Christian compassion for the weak individual instead of

tending to the health of the group, of the *Volk*. This partly Nietzschean position...included a rejection of the Christian principle of *caritas* or charity, and the Church's "commandment to
attend to the incurably ill person and render him medical aid
unto his death."[5]

The final words in quotation marks are those of Dr. Rudolf
Ramm, of the medical faculty of the University of Berlin. Dr.
Ramm helped guide German doctors away from caring for the
unfit, urging them not to think of themselves primarily as caretak-
ers of the sick, and certainly not as instruments of charity. Every
German doctor, he said, should be a "physician to the *Volk*," a "biological soldier."[6] To be a physician to the *Volk* meant (in the words
of Dr. Gerhard Wagner, chief physician of the Reich) to attend to
the "promotion and perfection of the health of the German people...to ensure that the people realize the full potential of their
racial and genetic endowment." Of course, as Dr. Ramm made
clear, this would mean preventing at all costs "bastardization" of the
race "through the propagation of unworthy and racially alien elements...and maintaining and increasing those of sound heredity"
for the sake of "keeping our blood pure."[7] This was the big picture
of Nazism, the "ideal" into which the extermination of the Jews fit.

Let us now turn to the master artist who painted such lurid colors. Hitler's first passion was painting (his first ambition was to
become an artist), but he soon saw a greater vision that he would
impress upon the canvas of history. We must therefore step back
and look at the whole canvas as he envisioned it in *Mein Kampf*. As
measured by its foul effects, it is one of the most evil books in history. Even the most liberal-minded would wish that this book had
never been published, and if published, its every word quickly
destroyed. Modern Germans feel the pain of its continued exis-

tence acutely, having awakened from a long night of barbarity and seen their own faces in a demon's mirror. In reading the available English translations, I found myself needing to consult the original German. Checking the cost with the online bookseller Amazon, I found a dire warning: "Cannot Be Shipped to Germany."

To grasp the whole horror of Hitler's book, we must resist the temptation to reduce the full measure of his crimes to one repugnant aspect, the destruction of the Jews. All too many, I'm afraid, who do make a go at reading *Mein Kampf* skip straight to the sections (primarily Volume I, Chapter XI) that contain the most lurid passages regarding the racial superiority of the Aryans and the racial inferiority of the Jews. Given the ghastliness of the Nazi atrocities against the Jews, such impatience at getting to Hitler's corrupt heart is understandable. We should, however, read the entire book from cover to cover (or at the very least, Volume I). It will then reveal itself for what it is: a book much like *The Prince*, a monumentally wicked book of very practical, very insightful advice for rulers whose entire goal is defined by earthly glory, and who are willing to make effectiveness, no matter how ruthless, their first principle.

Although Machiavelli obviously had the glory of Italy in mind, and especially Florence, his advice is offered to all who might heed his radical and revolutionary counsel. Hitler's advice, by contrast, is directed entirely to the earthly glory of Germany. But that is not so much a departure from Machiavelli as it is a profound solidification of the Machiavellian scheme.

Yet there is an interesting difference. While Machiavelli was the prince of practicality, turning away from all "idealism" to earthly *realpolitik*, there is something of the Platonist (however perverted) in Hitler. He saw himself as a visionary who beheld an ideal world peopled by an ideal humanity, a utopian vision that however unrealizable in practice should act as the pattern for ruthless political action.

Let's look more carefully at this often-overlooked aspect. Hitler makes an important distinction—again, one that runs all the way back to Plato—between the "political philosopher" (or in more literal translation, the "program-maker" [*Programmatiker*]) and the "practical political leader" [*Politiker*].[8] According to Hitler, the "task" of the political philosopher as the "guiding star to those who are looking about for light" is to "lay down the principles of a programme or policy." His goal is "the statement of the absolute truth," rather than an analysis of whether what he outlines is "expedient and practical." He considers "only the goal," and then "It is for the political leader to point out the way in which that goal may be reached."[9]

> The greatness of the one [the political philosopher or program-maker] will depend on the absolute truth of his idea, considered in the abstract; whereas that of the other [the political leader] will depend on whether or not he correctly judges the given realities and how they may be utilized under the guidance of the truths established by the former. The test of greatness as applied to a political leader is the success of his plans and his enterprises, which means his ability to reach the goal for which he sets out; whereas the final goal set up by the political philosopher can never be reached; for human thought may grasp truths and picture ends which it sees like clear crystal, though such ends can never be completely fulfilled because human nature is weak and imperfect. The more an idea is correct in the abstract, and, therefore, all the more powerful, the smaller is the possibility of putting it into practice, at least as far as this latter depends on human beings. The significance of a political philosopher does not

depend on the practical success of the plans he lays down but
rather on their absolute truth and the influence they exert on the
progress of mankind. If it were otherwise, the founders of reli-
gions could not be considered as the greatest men who have ever
lived, because their moral aims will never be completely or even
approximately carried out in practice. Even that religion which
is called the Religion of Love is really no more than a faint reflex
of the will of its sublime Founder. But its significance lies in the
orientation which it endeavoured to give to human civilization,
and human virtue and morals.[10]

Hitler then goes on to make another entirely Platonic point, that
the "very wide difference between the functions of a political
philosopher and a practical political leader is the reason why the
qualifications necessary for both functions are scarcely ever found
associated in the same person."[11] The divergence of functions is
due in part to the diverse demands on each: for the political
philosopher, the meditative demands of the theoretical life and its
need to abstract from the particularities to reach what is universal
and eternal; for the practical political leader, the agitated, practical
demands of the political life that must necessarily focus almost
exclusively on the particularities of daily life. Even more (as Plato
makes clear in *The Republic*), the divergence between the political
philosopher and the practical politician has its source in human
nature itself. The philosopher looks at what is "ideal," what human
nature would look like if its weaknesses were removed and it were
perfected; the practical politician must always work according to
what is practical, using "human nature" that is "weak and imperfect" as his material.

But, notes Hitler, "within long spans of human progress it may
occasionally happen that the practical politician and political

philosopher are one." When this occurs—what Plato had envisioned as the highly unlikely union of the philosopher and the king—there arises "the constructive political philosopher," who enters the ranks of the rare "genuinely great statesmen."[12] "The more intimate this union" between practical politician and political philosopher, "the greater will be the obstacles which the activity of the politician will have to encounter." The "greater the work" of this rare man, "the less will he be appreciated by his contemporaries. His struggle [*kampf*] will accordingly be all the more severe, and his success all the rarer."[13]

That struggle is the *kampf* of Hitler's title. Hitler took himself to be that rarest of things, the union of philosopher and king, political philosopher and practical political leader, program-maker and politician in one. Put this way, Hitler seems almost noble, until we realize that the philosophy to which he ascribed was an amalgam of Machiavelli, Darwin, Schopenhauer, and Nietzsche (as mixed with the racial theories of the Frenchman Joseph-Arthur, comte de Gobineau). We might say that whatever hesitations to action one finds in Darwin, Schopenhauer, or even Nietzsche, Hitler casts aside with the ruthlessness of Machiavelli.

One must also add that, however profoundly evil his intellectual antecedents, Hitler's own philosophical abilities were modest, exhibiting all the marks of an especially rank philosophical popularizer. If we may characterize him as an evil genius, his genius was largely borrowed while the evil was characteristically his own. As we can see from those whose genius he borrowed, Hitler's philosophy was a practical culmination of modern atheism invested with quasi-religious fervor. This, I believe, accounts for Hitler's ambiguous stance toward religion: cold, anti-clerical, and acerbic while also fanatically warm and inviting. Sometimes he speaks as an enemy to Christianity, sometimes as a friend (rather like Machiavelli, for both men view religion as a tool of the practical politician, to be discarded or repudiated when inconvenient and embraced when useful). In regard to understanding his ultimate stance toward religion, rather than stacking up pro and con quotes to see which pile is largest, we can examine the arguments Hitler makes in *Mein Kampf* and make our judgments accordingly. (I suggest reading Michael Burleigh's astute analysis of all the ambiguities of Hitler's attitude toward religion in *Sacred Causes*.[14])

As noted, Hitler's original aim was not to become involved in politics, but rather to be a painter and then an architect. Yet from a very early time, as he himself relates, he was fired by nationalism. In school, besides art, history was his "favorite subject." Set ablaze by his history teacher, Leopold Poetsch, he was filled with "national fervor" and "then and there became a young rebel."[15] Hitler became a youthful advocate of the German Empire of Otto von Bismarck, and he would eventually fight, and be wounded, for the Second Reich in World War I.

After the death of both his parents, Hitler moved from his childhood home in Braunau am Inn, Austria, to Vienna to study architecture. Vienna was the liberal, cosmopolitan city of Sigmund Freud and had a large Jewish population. There in Vienna, living in poverty among the lowest class, Hitler had his "eyes . . . opened to two perils . . . Marxism and Judaism."[16] We shall come back to these "two perils" soon enough. But first we must understand that Hitler's firsthand experience of poverty kindled in him great sympathy for the poor, as he makes clear in his account of his Vienna years:

> The Vienna manual labourers lived in surroundings of appalling misery. I shudder even today when I think of the woeful dens in which people dwelt, the night shelters and the slums, and all the tenebrous spectacles of ordure, loathsome filth and wickedness.

What will happen one day when hordes of emancipated slaves [manual laborers] come forth from these dens of misery to swoop down on their unsuspecting fellow men? For this other world [of the bourgeoisie] does not think about such a possibility. They have allowed these things to go on without caring and even without suspecting—in their total lack of instinctive understanding—that sooner or later destiny will take its vengeance unless it will have been appeased in time.[17]

Hitler's experience of the ill effects of capitalism brought him to throw his energies into socialism. He became a member of the German Workers' Party, soon to be renamed the National Socialist German Workers' Party, or Nazi Party for short.

But even before joining up, Hitler believed that the social problems he witnessed in Vienna needed a radical, even ruthless solution to effect true change. As he says with breathtaking concision, "the sentimental attitude would be the wrong one to adopt:"

Even in those days I already saw that there was a two-fold method by which alone it would be possible to bring about an amelioration of these conditions. This method is: first, to create better fundamental conditions of social development by establishing a profound feeling for social responsibilities among the public; second, to combine this feeling for social responsibilities with a ruthless determination to prune away all excrescences which are incapable of being improved.

Just as Nature concentrates its greatest attention, not to the maintenance of what already exists but on the selective breeding of offspring in order to carry on the species, so in human life also it is less a matter of artificially improving the existing generation—which, owing to human characteristics, is impossible in ninety-nine cases out of a hundred—and more a matter of securing from the very start a better road for future development.

During my struggle for existence in Vienna I perceived very clearly that the end of all social activity must never be merely sentimental charity, which is ridiculous and useless, but it must rather be a means to find a way of eliminating the fundamental deficiencies which necessarily bring about the degradation of the individual or at least lead him towards such degradation.[18]

Great humanitarian goals; ruthless means to achieve them; going against humanity to help humanity. Hitler assures the reader that such means are necessary, because while the upper classes have a "sense of guilt" that they "permitted this tragedy of degradation," this guilt paralyzes "every effort at making a serious and firm decision to act," creating people who are "timid and half-hearted." For the sake of curing the problems that ail society, there can be no half-hearted solutions. Guilt must be put aside: "When the individual is no longer burdened with his own consciousness of blame in this regard, then and only then will he have that inner tranquility and outer force to cut off drastically and ruthlessly all the parasite growth and root out the weeds."[19]

The guilt for the degradation of the lower classes must be placed elsewhere. We may now turn again to the twin perils of Judaism and Marxism. Hitler chastised the industrialists, the bourgeoisie, for creating the grinding poverty of the lower classes and then ignoring it. Hitler believed that because the Jews were the true power behind commerce, they were ultimately to be blamed for oppressing the poor. By ignoring these woeful conditions, the bourgeoisie were creating in the oppressed the predisposition to join the Marxists, who were everywhere fomenting rebellion out of discontent. Of course, Hitler assures the reader, Marxism was also essentially a Jewish intrigue, carried forth under the auspices of the German Social Democratic Party. The whole situation, then, was a two-sided Jewish conspiracy,[20] its goal the creation of the conditions in which the Jews could break down nation-based power and take over the world, replacing the true *Volk* with a Jewish state.

In order to understand Hitler's antagonism to Jews, we must also grasp his romanticism of race (which, I think it is fair to say, is the real source of his religious fervor). As Hitler made clear, "the highest aim of human existence is not the maintenance of a State or Government but rather the conservation of the race."[21] The deepest problem with Jewish capitalism and Jewish Marxism, as Hitler saw it, was the Jews' united, conspiratorial antagonism to nationalism. Hitler viewed nations as a racial entities, biologically based societies. In being increasingly internationalized, capitalism works against the primary good of the nation, and in creating a large, disgruntled oppressed class, turns citizens bound by race against each other.[22] Marxism looks for the destruction of every state, and hence attacks nations as merely bourgeois structures of oppression that must be destroyed.[23] Jewish capitalism and Jewish Marxism were therefore undermining Germany's racial greatness from two sides.

Racial greatness should have been fully expressed in 1871, when Otto von Bismarck formed the Second Reich, uniting for the first time a congeries of separate states into the German nation. But Hitler believed Germany's unified greatness was only partially expressed in the Second Reich because the forces of "inner degeneration had already set in . . . when the united Empire was formed and the German nation began to make rapid external progress."[24] The degeneration was the result of the Jews, race-mixing, and the rise of Jewish capitalism and its concomitant Jewish Marxism. One of the questions that haunted Hitler—why the Second Reich lost World War I—suddenly had an answer. Germany did not lose the war on the battlefield; "the most profound and decisive cause [of its defeat] must be attributed to the lack of insight into the racial problem and especially in the failure to recognize the Jewish danger."[25]

The Jews could be blamed for nearly every evil: from the humiliating defeat of the Second Reich in World War I and the postwar Bolshevik upheavals to the decadence of the Weimar Republic to the economic crisis of the Great Depression. The only thing to be done was create another Reich, another glorious empire, one in which the Jewish problem, as well as all other social problems, would be solved.

To undertake such an enormous task, Hitler laid out his political first principles in *Mein Kampf.* He rejected the notion of liberal contract theory (found in Thomas Hobbes and especially in John Locke), the idea that the state arises "from a compact made between contracting parties within a certain limited territory, for the purpose of serving economic needs."[26] The state is primarily a racial unit, argued Hitler, not an economic union; it is rooted in biology, not commercial utility. "The State is a community of living beings who have kindred physical and spiritual natures, organized for the purpose of assuring the conservation of their own kind and to help towards fulfilling those ends which Providence has assigned to that particular race or racial branch. Therein and therein alone lie the purpose and meaning of a State."[27]

Hitler's rejection of the economically defined state was not merely the result of romantic racism. It is, he argues, a return to the true roots of the state, for "States have always arisen from the instinct to maintain the racial group."[28] When commerce becomes the primary concern of the state, it creates feckless citizens whose highest good is material prosperity and pleasure. Such citizens make bad soldiers: a man "will die for an ideal but not for a business."[29] For "as soon as man is called upon to struggle for purely material causes he will avoid death as best he can; for death and the enjoyment of the material fruits of a victory are quite incompatible concepts.... And only the will to save the race and native land or the State, which offers protection to the race, has in all ages been the urge which has forced men to face the weapons of their enemies."[30] Hobbesian-utilitarian man, the man of modern liberalism who counts pleasure as the highest good and pain as the highest evil, lives only for his own pleasure and preservation. But the Reich needs men willing to die in battle. Without such heroic courage, the new German Empire could not be realized.

In order to galvanize the German people, Hitler realized that he needed to place before them a new *Weltanschauung,* or religio-political ideal, "an entirely new spiritual order of things" that could defeat the existing commercial-cosmopolitan worldview of liberalism sapping Germany of its strength.[31] It was precisely the "lack of a definite and uniformly accepted *Weltanschauung* and the general uncertainty of outlook consequent on that lack" that had caused the Second Reich's "final collapse."[32] The old *Weltanschauung* of liberalism that destroyed the Second Reich "can never be broken by the use of force...except on one condition: namely, that this use of force is in the service of a new idea or *Weltanschauung* which burns with a new flame." This *Weltanschauung* "must receive the stamp of a definite political faith."[33]

This new spiritual order of things Hitler hoped to set in flame must (to recall Nietzsche) inculcate a spiritualization of cruelty that, going beyond conventional notions of good and evil, allows for the ruthlessness needed to achieve the necessary solutions to poverty and Germany's other social problems. Hitler brilliantly solves the

problem of bad conscience in the use of ruthless force by spiritu-
alizing the Darwinian law of nature as "Providential:"

> Man must not fall into the error of thinking that he was ever meant
> to become lord and master of Nature.... Man must realize that a
> fundamental law of necessity reigns throughout the realm of
> Nature and that his existence is subject to the law of eternal strug-
> gle and strife. He will then feel that there cannot be a separate law
> for mankind in a world in which planets and suns follow their
> orbits, where moons and planets trace their destined paths, where
> the strong are always the masters of the weak and where those sub-
> ject to such laws must obey them or be destroyed. Man must also
> submit to the eternal principles of this supreme wisdom.[34]

We may now see why it is that Hitler would so often appear to
drape his brutality with spiritual language; that is, we may now
understand why Hitler often appears to be religious (just as Machiavelli would recommend). A *Weltanschauung* is both religious and
political;[35] it is a "political faith" that entails the use of spiritual
energies for political ends. As we've seen, modernity from Machiavelli, Descartes, and Hobbes forward bequeaths to its posterity the
merely material man. But man so defined will not sacrifice his
material comfort, and certainly not his own life, for the good of the
nation. Religion becomes necessary amidst the general historical
secularization of the West because materialism alone proves insuf-
ficient as a motive for unified political action. Hence the flourishing of political faiths in the twentieth century, the faith being
entirely defined by the political.

On a deeper level, Hitler took religion to be necessary as a
means to control and direct the masses precisely because they are
incapable of understanding philosophy. As Hitler says:

> This human world of ours would be inconceivable without the practical existence of a religious belief. The great masses of a nation are not composed of philosophers. For the masses of people especially, faith is absolutely the only basis of a moral outlook on life. The various substitutes that have been offered have not shown any results that might warrant us in thinking that they might usefully replace the existing denominations [of Christianity in Germany]. . . . Until such a substitute [for religion] be available only fools and criminals would think of abolishing the existing religion.[36]

Of course, Hitler's moral outlook on life was a quasi-Nietzschean form of spiritualized Darwinism. Christianity was useful as long as it supported Hitler's program. Liberal Christianity, with its flexible doctrine and morality and emphasis on curing social ills, could be particularly useful. But conservative Christianity—with its dogmatic claims and moral commandments, as expressed in such actions as the Catholic Church's opposition to eugenics—was to be attacked whenever it contradicted the regime. The real religion of the Reich was not Christianity, but the Wagnerian mystical Germanism that so entranced Nietzsche.

We shouldn't think that an atheist like Nietzsche would have no use for religion. As he stated in *Beyond Good and Evil,*

> The philosopher as *we* understand him . . . will make use of religions for his project of cultivation and education, just as he will make use of whatever political and economic states are at hand. . . . For the strong and independent who are prepared and predestined to command and in whom the reason and art of a governing race become incarnate, religion is one more means for overcoming resistances, for the ability to rule—as a bond that

unites rulers and subjects and betrays and delivers the consciences of the latter, that which is most concealed and intimate
and would like to elude obedience, to the former. ...

To ordinary human beings, finally—the vast majority who
exist for service and the general advantage, and who *may* exist
only for that—religion gives an inestimable contentment with
their situation and type, manifold peace of the heart, an
ennobling of obedience. ... Religion and religious significance
spread the splendor of the sun over such ever-toiling human
beings and make their own sight tolerable to them.[37]

This principle was understood all too well by Hitler. The Nazi
Party would be victorious in the "gigantic struggle ... only if it succeeded from the very outset in awakening a sacrosanct conviction
in the hearts of its followers," and this would take not "a new elec-
toral slogan ... but ... an entirely new *Weltanschauung*."[38] This new
worldview, or as he very exactly calls it, "political faith,"[39] will be
a union of Darwin and Nietzsche. It will be based on a kind of folk
religion, that is, a religion of the racially defined *Volk*, a worship of
the Germanic race as the only one capable of eliminating the weak
and bringing the *übermensch* into existence in accordance with the
cruelties of Nature. Hitler's words all too clearly portend the atrocities to come when the Nazis gained power:

[T]he *völkisch* concept of the world recognizes that the primordial
racial elements are of the greatest significance for mankind. In
principle, the State is looked upon only as a means to an end and
this end is the conservation of the racial characteristics of mankind.
Therefore on the *völkisch* principle we cannot admit that one race
is equal to another. By recognizing that they are different, the
völkisch concept separates mankind into races of superior and

inferior quality. On the basis of this recognition it feels bound, in conformity with the eternal Will that dominates the universe, to postulate the victory of the better and stronger and the subordination of the inferior and weaker. And so it pays homage to the truth that the principle underlying all Nature's operations is the aristocratic principle and it believes that this law holds good even down to the last individual organism.... The *völkisch* belief holds that humanity must have its ideals, because ideals are a necessary condition of human existence itself. But, on the other hand, it denies that an ethical ideal has the right to prevail if it endangers the existence of a race that is the standard-bearer of a higher ethical ideal. For in a world which would be composed of mongrels and negroids all ideals of human beauty and nobility and all hopes of an idealized future for our humanity would be lost forever.

On this planet of ours human culture and civilization are indissolubly bound up with the presence of the Aryan. If he should be exterminated or subjugated, then the dark shroud of a new barbarian era would enfold the earth....

Hence the folk concept of the world is in profound accord with Nature's will; because it restores the free play of the forces which will lead the race through stages of sustained reciprocal education towards a higher type, until finally the best portion of mankind will possess the earth and will be free to work in every domain all over the world and even reach spheres that lie outside the earth.[40]

As we now know all too clearly, in going beyond good and evil by defining good and evil according to what would produce the Aryan *übermensch*, Hitler ushered in "the dark shroud of a new barbarian era." Let no one ever doubt the evil that one man's book can do. But what is that evil? There is in Hitler the morbid culmination of an essentially modern immoderation: the desire to fix everything once and for all according to some utopian plan. Hitler began with the admirable desire to fix the social problem of poverty. He soon designed a plan to fix all social problems. And he ended with the Final Solution: the elimination of all those he believed were causing the problems. He is a case study in the infernal end to which immoderate good intentions continually lead.

Why? What's wrong with immoderation for the sake of a good cause? Well, to begin with, immoderation rejects the reality of sin. If I understand that there is something deeply warped in my own soul, then I realize that this warp will inevitably manifest itself in my vision of things, no matter how grand or humanitarian it is. I will not, then, impose by force the reality of my sin upon the reality of the world. Hitler's grand vision, his *Weltanschauung*, was not a *world*-view—as it didn't correspond to the real world—but the warp of his darkly sinful soul writ large. There is a reason why moderation is a classical and Christian virtue.

A Christian or Jew should also embrace the humble recognition that he is not God. The first of the Ten Commandments—thou shalt have no other gods—is first of all directed to *us*. Hitler, and many other modern dictators, put themselves in the place of God. Part of the warp in Hitler's soul was the belief that he had seen the entire truth about the Jews from his experience in Vienna, from reading the scientifically worthless racial theorists touting the glories of the Aryans, and absorbing the Darwinism that was so forcibly preached in German universities and the popular press. He wanted to believe that the Jews were the cause of every evil— not only because he had a sinful hatred of the Jews but also because he needed some single simple thing that caused all evil, real or imagined, that he, like some omniscient, omnipotent deity, could remove. He wanted to be the savior of humanity and ended up being its most infamous excrescence of evil.

But the significant influence on Hitler of thinkers such as Darwin and Nietzsche should bring us to the recognition that we can't hold Hitler up as some kind of singular exemplar of evil. He was a man of his times, a nineteenth-and twentieth-century man, who owed as much as Margaret Sanger to the Darwinian eugenic theories in circulation and shared the same reaction as Nietzsche to the Epicurean diminution of man brought about by the liberalism of Hobbes and Mill. If it were not so, he could not have gathered so many willing participants in the monumental wickedness of the Third Reich from the German intelligentsia. Even more telling, if we treat Hitler as some kind of curious exception, we will smooth over the continuity between the eugenic fantasies of the Nazis and our own. Hitler's extermination of the unfit was not just limited to the Jews; the slaughter of the Jews was only one aspect of his overall eugenic vision. While we shun racial extermination of unfit children and adults in gas chambers, we have very little anxiety about eliminating the very same kind of less-than-perfect human beings in abortion clinics.

CHAPTER TWELVE

The Future
of an Illusion
(1927)

> "[I]t would be very nice if there were a God who created
> the world and was a benevolent Providence, . . . a moral order
> in the universe and an after-life; but it is a very striking fact
> that all this is exactly as we are bound to wish it to be. . . ."
>
> Sigmund Freud (1856–1939)

SIGMUND FREUD WAS, BY HIS OWN PROUD AND ACCURATE DESCRIPtion, a "godless Jew." When he was still young, his family moved from Czechoslovakia to Vienna, a liberal haven for Jews in the latter half of the nineteenth century. The Freuds' Jewishness was at most cultural, never religious, but the Christian-based anti-Semitism Freud encountered perhaps confirmed his animosity to all religion, especially Christianity. *The Future of an Illusion* was his revenge.

The Future of an Illusion is a fundamental attack on religion, dismissing it as mere illusion, foolish wish-fulfillment by infantile minds. Freud's ideas were not wholly original; he built on an intellectual structure of atheism that began with Machiavelli and reached its philosophical culmination in Nietzsche. Freud provided a new variation on the theme by taking atheism for granted. It was, in his imagination, simply true. Rejecting the idea that religion exists because God exists and that human beings therefore have a natural propensity to worship, Freud believed that he had to give another explanation for religion. But even from an atheist's standpoint, Freud's explanation is bizarre. First given full sail in his *Totem and Taboo* (1913), Freud's theory was that the origin of the religious cult (the origin of *cult*ure) was the killing and eating of a father by his sons. And why would sons want to murder their father? Because, naturally, they desired to have sex with their mother. In true primitive fashion, they believed that by eating their father they gained his strength and privileges. Nevertheless, they did feel guilt, which at first they repressed, but then expressed through sacred meals that simultaneously commemorated, condemned, and covered up the original gruesome patricidal feast. This sacred meal in turn became the foundation of religion and its moral prohibition of incest and patricide.

There it is. Look into our dark past, Freud maintained, and we find in the branches of our family tree incest, patricide, and cannibalism. Of course, he had no more evidence for such an original immoral free-for-all than Hobbes or Rousseau had for their entirely fictional accounts of the state of nature. And it's not too difficult to see why Hobbes in particular has been called the father of Freud. As we recall, Hobbes painted his anti-Edenic picture of the state of nature as utterly amoral, with no natural good or evil. Human beings, therefore, had the right to anything and everything, even the right to patricide, incest, and cannibalism if they so desired. Hobbes's denial of good and evil followed directly upon his atheism, for if good and evil existed by nature, then some intelligent moral being would have to be the cause. Inheriting Hobbes's atheism, Freud filled in the details of his entirely fictitious state of nature by adding a dash of Rousseau, in particular Rousseau's emphasis on the aimless, indiscriminate, and amoral libidinous impulses of pre-social man. "Savages are not evil," we recall Rousseau saying, "precisely because they do not know what it is to be good." Thus, no sexual impulse—even incest—could be evil for our primitive ancestors. (We'll soon see more of Rousseau in Freud.)

Freud's rooting of religion in incest and patricide was a direct attack not only on religion as a whole, but especially on Christianity—both on the Eucharist and perhaps on the idea of the Virgin Mary—with his implication that the most holy sacrament of the Christian Church was a vile recapitulation of patricidal cannibalism fueled by incest. We cannot forget Nietzsche's assumption that religion was an entirely human creation. Since Freud read Nietzsche, this may have done as much as anything to help form his presentation of religion in *The Future of an Illusion*. Yet we cannot blame Nietzsche for everything; the notion that religion was a mere human creation can be found all the way back in Machiavelli. And Freud seemed to need little prodding. He was a pugilistic atheist, as biographer Peter Gay characterizes him. "To demolish religion with psychoanalytic weapons," Gay remarks, "had been on Freud's agenda for many years."[1] It is unsurprising, then, that *The Future of an Illusion* expresses (in Freud's own words) "my absolutely negative attitude toward religion, in every form and dilution."[2]

We do not want to give the impression, however, that Freud was all bad. He did immensely rich work in psychoanalysis that helped unearth some of the deep, unconscious motivations of human action. But, unfortunately, his atheistic assumptions poisoned much of the fruit. It is one thing to discover the great distance that sometimes divides our conscious motives and actions from unconscious or repressed psychic damage or desires. It is quite another to assume, as Freud did, that there is amoral anarchy at the very bottom of our souls, and that morality itself is an entirely artificial suppression of our quite natural desire to kill for pleasure. We see, then, the result of Freud's rejection of religion, and in particular his animosity against Judaism and Christianity: his rebellion took the form of baptizing as natural the most hideously unnatural sins, sins condemned by every society as the most unholy and unthinkable.

Moreover, like his fellow rebels Hobbes and Rousseau, Freud damned as unnatural the Christian-based morality of Western society. He began with the Hobbesian assumption that human beings are essentially anti-social, or perhaps more accurately, anti-civil. As human beings are naturally—not sinfully—lazy and passion-driven, and "every civilization rests on a compulsion to work and a renunciation of instinct," then "every individual is virtually an enemy of civilization." Even after we are "civilized," because we still have these original amoral instincts, we all suffer under the inevitable "frustration" that comes from suppressing their satisfaction.[3]

Just what are these original instincts that "still form the kernel of hostility to civilization"? Well, as we've already noted, Freud states famously that, "Among these instinctual wishes are those of incest, cannibalism, and lust for killing."[4] That's what all of us would do if we didn't repress these natural desires. Witness the wistful Hobbesian reverie Freud offers at the beginning of the third chapter of *The Future of an Illusion*:

> We have spoken of the hostility to civilization which is produced by the pressure that civilization demands. If one imagines its prohibitions lifted—if, then, one may take any woman one pleases as a sexual object, if one may without hesitation kill one's rival for her love or anyone else who stands in one's way, if, too, one can carry off any of the other man's belongings without asking leave—how splendid, what a string of satisfactions one's life would be! True, one soon comes across the first difficulty: every-

one else has exactly the same wishes as I have and will treat me with no more consideration than I treat him. And so in reality only one person could be made unrestrictedly happy by such a removal of the restrictions of civilization, and he would be a tyrant, a dictator, who had seized all the means to power....

But how ungrateful, how short-sighted after all, to strive for the abolition of civilization! What would then remain would be a state of nature, and that would be far harder to bear.[5]

We can see in these words that for all the claims of Freud's originality, he is ultimately indebted to Hobbes for his assumptions and also to those who followed Hobbes's lead. (And to be fair to Freud, he realized that what he was saying had already been proclaimed by "other and better men" who stated it "in a much more complete, forcible, and impressive manner."[6]) We are also not surprised, given the length of the pedigree of this view and the centuries it had to seep into the soil of the West and poison it, that the notions of the holy criminal and anti-social hero would eventually take hold of the intelligentsia and hence the popular imagination.

Freud's originality was his embedding of the Hobbesian view into the discipline of psychology. He claimed that psychological disorders were the result of the unnatural repression of our naturally unholy and anti-social desires, and that some people just couldn't handle the repression: "neurotics... react to these frustrations with asocial behaviour."[7] The irony of Freud's position should be evident: We are naturally asocial; civilization is frustrating; neurotics react to this unnatural frustration by asocial behavior. Therefore, neurotics are the only sane people because they react to unnatural frustration by trying to reclaim their original, natural, asocial and amoral state. The result: the anti-social psychopath who kills without conscience is the most natural of all. The interesting effect of Freud's proclamation that evil is natural was the seemingly unintended consequence of making psychopathic insanity natural.

Of course, it is not difficult to see Rousseau peeking through Freud here. The obvious result of declaring in the *First* and *Second Discourse* that society is unnatural (as Rousseau made clear in his follow-up book, *The Social Contract*) was that the "artificial" confines of society could only be seen as chains. "Man was born free," thundered Rousseau, "and everywhere he is in chains."[8] But as did Rousseau, even while creating a longing for this natural state in which the unholiest desires ran free, Freud tried to reconcile us to the slavery of society. That is the one of the problems he sought to solve in his *The Future of an Illusion.*

Freud's attempt to reconcile Hobbesian-Rousseauian man to the chains of society as a solution depends upon his assumption that we are all such men. No matter how sober, rational, and compelling his solution to the problem, we must always keep in mind that his solution is only as good as his framing of the problem, his answer only as good as the question.

I point this out precisely because of an enduring difficulty besetting human nature, made ten thousand times worse by the printing press. There are all kinds of seemingly sober, rational, and compelling cures for ailments that either don't exist or that are woefully misdiagnosed. As with all quacks and their cures, the administering empiric is usually empirical enough to have at least one foot on semi-solid ground. The quack therefore sounds authoritative (especially to himself), but in truth, the wonderfully logical solution he offers to the patient often has the insalubrious effect of killing him. There is nothing more reasonable, more logical, than bleeding someone who is deathly ill if his illness really is the result of excess bile in the blood. As we now know, the practice of bleeding patients for every imaginable ailment, while considered impeccably logical for centuries among physicians, was based on peccable assumptions about good and bad humors in the blood. Thus good logic produced rueful results, more often than not the protracted illness or death of the patient. For this reason we must always keep Freud's assumptions in mind as we listen to his "solution of the problem of religion."[9]

I realize that I just said that the problem Freud set out to solve was that of reconciling us to the artificial chains of society. That remains true, and it is still his fundamental problem. Religion becomes a problem because it was, in Freud's view, the original solution to the fundamental problem, and since it is ultimately the wrong solution, it too has become a problem. Let's sort this out, recalling what we said above about Freud's unsavory view of our "natural" or "original" state.

The first assumption Freud makes, as we know, is that God doesn't exist. Again, it is no secret that Freud did not want God to exist. His wish formed his fundamental assumption. Therefore, the existence of God becomes something that needs to be explained according to something other than the existence of God. Freud chose "the child's helplessness" and then "the helplessness of the adult which continues it."[10] Helpless before what? In regard to what? A feeling of helplessness "against the crushingly superior force of nature."[11]

Interesting assumption, but how do we know it's true? Freud attempts to affirm it with an analogy to childhood, in which "the mother, who satisfies the child's hunger, becomes its first love-object, and certainly also its first protection against all the undefined dangers which threaten it in the external world—its first protection against anxiety, we may say."

In this function [of protection] the mother is soon replaced by the stronger father, who retains that position for the rest of childhood. But the child's attitude to its father is coloured by a peculiar ambivalence. The father himself constitutes a danger for the child, perhaps because of its earlier relation to its mother. Thus it fears him no less than it longs for him and admires him.... When the growing individual finds that he is destined to remain a child for ever... [because] he can never do without protection against strange superior powers, he lends those powers the features belonging to the figure of his father; he creates for himself the gods whom he dreads, whom he seeks to propitiate, and whom he nevertheless entrusts with his own protection. Thus his longing for a father is a motive identical with his need for protection against the consequences of his human weakness.[12]

Such is the real beginning of religion, and the previous loopy Oedipal ruminations mentioned above from *Totem and Taboo* are then tacked on. The smallest of children are fundamentally sexual, and therefore the mother-attachment arouses incestuous sexual desires in the child; the child then sees the father as a sexual rival, and desires to kill him even while admiring him as the strong protector. And so the child kills and eats his father, but then in a conscious-stricken inner *disputandum de gustibus*, the child decides to hide his crime by deifying his father and sublimating his crime through a sacred totem meal (consisting of a sacrificial animal, which is used after the first family meal to represent the father).

Most of this speculation was impure fantasy, a bizarre projection of Freud's fundamental wish that religion be discredited by the most salacious conjectures he could conjure. As biographer Peter Gay remarks:

[T]he flaws compromising the argument of *Totem and Taboo* emerged more and more obtrusively [as they were scrutinized]— except to Freud's most uncritical acolytes. Cultural anthropologists demonstrated that while some totemic tribes practice the ritual of the sacrificial totem meal, most of them do not; what Robertson Smith [upon whom Freud heavily relied] had thought the essence of totemism turned out to be an exception. Again, the conjectures [upon which Freud relied] of Darwin and others about the prehistoric horde governed autocratically by a polygamous and monopolistic male did not stand up well to further research, especially the kind of research among the higher primates that had not been available when Freud wrote *Totem and Taboo*. Freud's stirring portrayal of that lethal fraternal rebellion against patriarch seemed increasingly implausible.[13]

Contrary evidence from experts didn't bother Freud or his devout disciples, however. His wish that his theory be vindicated had determined his use of the experts to begin with. "What he wanted from the experts," notes Gay, "was corroboration; he pounced on their arguments when they sustained his own, disregarded them when they did not."[14] In a spectacularly uncritical and hence revealing outburst written near his life's end, Freud defended his cherry-picking of evidence and his obstinate refusal to accept the ever-mounting counter-evidence gathered by ethnologists against his theses: "I am not an ethnologist, but a psychoanalyst. I had the *right* to pick out of the ethnological literature what I could use for my analytical work."[15]

Dwelling on the curiously unscientific foundation of Freud's arguments in *Totem and Taboo* is obviously important for our assessment of his follow-up work, *The Future of an Illusion*. It makes us all the more wary of accepting his assumptions and his claims that they are somehow essentially rational or scientific. This is especially important when we examine Freud's definition of an illusion, as he considered religion to be a problem, in part, because it is an illusion.

> An illusion is not the same thing as an error; nor is it necessarily an error.... What is characteristic of illusions is that they are derived from human wishes. In this respect they come near to psychiatric delusions.... Illusions need not necessarily be false— that is to say, unrealizable or in contradiction to reality.... Examples of illusions which have proved true [however] are not easy to find.... Thus we call a belief an illusion when a wish-fulfillment is a prominent factor in its motivation, and in doing so we disregard its relations to reality, just as the illusion itself sets no store by verification.[16]

Freud believed that he had demonstrated "the psychical origins of religious ideas" in "the terrifying...helplessness in childhood [that] aroused the need for protection—for protection through love—which was provided by the father," and that religious ideas are therefore "illusions, fulfillments of the oldest, strongest, and most urgent wishes of mankind." The illusion consists in the desire that there be a cosmic father who continues to allay our feeling of helplessness, taking care of us in this world and the next. But as God doesn't exist, this desire has no real object; it is not only an illusion, but a "delusion."[17] Religion is a creation of wish-fulfillment with no possibility of fulfillment:

> We shall tell ourselves that it would be very nice if there were a God who created the world and was a benevolent Providence, and if there were a moral order in the universe and an after-life; but it is a very striking fact that all this is exactly as we are bound

to wish it to be. And it would be more remarkable still if our wretched, ignorant and downtrodden ancestors had succeeded in solving all these difficult riddles of the universe.[18]

The rational thing to do, Freud asserts, is to give up this illusion. Grow up. Drop religion and embrace science. Become "irreligious in the truest sense of the word" and admit "man's insignificance or impotence in the face of the universe."[19]

But if there's no God, where did morality come from? The same place we got religion, says Freud. Divine prohibitions fictitiously ascribed to an infinitely magnified father were historically the source of moral order: "the killing of the primitive father…evoked an irresistible emotional reaction with momentous consequences. From it arose the commandment: thou shalt not kill."[20]

If we get rid of God, won't we just revert back to the primitive amoral free-for-all? Perhaps the scientific folk might behave. But won't the unscientific and unwashed masses, once they hear there's no one upstairs, run riot?

Well, said Freud, it's worth the gamble because humanity has, more or less, reached the age of reason and it's high time we leave the illusions of childhood behind and embrace reason. We don't need to ground morality in God. We'll have a purely rational foundation for morality instead, basically that of Hobbes. You'd like to kill everyone, but you realize that everyone else would like to kill everyone else, including you, so everyone decides not to kill anyone else.[21] There you go, a God-free "thou shalt not kill."

But what about those divine rewards and punishments? What will happen without heaven and hell? What will become of us once we have nothing to look forward to after death but nothingness?

When we are no longer under the confusion about the source of moral order, we will have to give up the illusion that there is an extension of the moral order into eternity. But this, Freud avers, may very well have beneficial effects: "By withdrawing their expectations from the other world and concentrating all their liberated energies into their life on earth, they will probably succeed in achieving a state of things in which life will become tolerable for everyone and civilization no longer oppressive to anyone."[22]

A nice wish. And as Freud himself assumes that wishes are at the core of illusions, he candidly admits at the end, "I know how difficult it is to avoid illusions; perhaps the hopes I have confessed to are of an illusory nature, too." But "my illusions are not, like religious ones, incapable of correction. They have not the character of a delusion. If experience should show—not to me, but to others after me, who think as I do—that we have been mistaken, we will give up our expectations."[23]

Freud lived through World War I, but died on the eve of World War II. If he had lived to see liberated energy turned to godless savagery by Hitler, would he have given up his illusion as delusion? Or would he have ignored all the counter-evidence, just as he denied all the counter-evidence to his presentation of religion? Would Stalin have been enough? Mao? Pol Pot? How much evidence does a man of science need to give up a cherished illusion? The greatest crimes in the history of mankind came not from those in thrall to the "illusion" of Judaism and Christianity, but from those who claimed to be atheistic, scientific socialists. Yet despite this abominable evidence, Freud's fairy tale account of religion remains, for all too many, a grand illusion too compelling to give up.

CHAPTER THIRTEEN

Coming of Age in Samoa
(1928)

"The child of the future must have an open mind. The home must cease to plead an ethical cause or a religious belief with smiles or frowns, caresses or threats. The children must be taught how to think, not what to think. . . . "

Margaret Mead (1901–1978)

IN 1925, A VERY YOUNG GRADUATE STUDENT IN ANTHROPOLOGY, Margaret Mead, sailed to the island of Tau in American Samoa to test a rather interesting hypothesis: whether adolescent rebellion, turmoil, and angst were natural or cultural. Mead published her findings in 1928, adding to a swelling pile of confusion that included Margaret Sanger's *The Pivot of Civilization* (1922) and its faith in the liberating power of our sexual glands, Adolf Hitler's *Mein Kampf* (1925) and its identification of the Jews as the greatest problem facing genetic progress, and Sigmund Freud's *The Future of an Illusion* (1927), and its assertion that we are by nature amoral savages and that morality is only a series of taboos erected by man in the name of religion (itself an illusion). The inter-war years were indeed good times for bad books that added immensely to the West's treasury of pseudo-science. Mead's contribution was to foist on the poor Polynesian Samoans her own vision of a happy sexual paradise in *Coming of Age in Samoa.*

Mead's modus operandi of gathering "facts" from primitive fictions to suit her philosophical fancies has, as we've seen, a distinguished pedigree. Hobbes painted a vivid picture of our natural condition based entirely upon such a fiction. Rousseau and Freud did the same. All these authors used selective or imagined evidence to argue that human nature was best understood in man's primitive state. Their underlying assumption can be expressed in a simple formula: the natural = the primitive = the good. Whether the savage be noble or ignoble, a cheerful imp or a brutal beast, he was the Adam in whose image our nature was first formed, and whose image we must recover for inspection by scrubbing off the accretions of civilization.

I use the name "Adam" purposely, since as we've seen one of the preoccupations of modernity, especially its most secularizing spirits, is the endless attempt to conjure a counter-myth to the Genesis account found in the Bible. When Hobbes, Rousseau, or Freud imagined man's pre-civilized state, they did so not on the basis of historical evidence, but on supposition. Underlying that supposition was a belief that what is natural and original is best. This is true even for Thomas Hobbes, whose state of nature was a state of war, for even though we escape from this nasty condition into civil society, we always wish that we could still do anything and get anything we want.

Margaret Mead did try to find a living example of the human primitive, but her famous portrait of the carefree, libidinous Samoans was in fact just one more modern fiction—and this would have been true even if the Samoans were exactly as she described them in *Coming of Age in Samoa.* (Her findings are now a matter of scholarly dispute.)

Mead's quest was flawed from the beginning, because even if a "primitive people" are carefree and libidinous, one cannot infer that simply because they appear more primitive that they are somehow closer to what is natural and good, and can therefore provide a corrective to our own way of life. They might be both more primitive and more perverse. Their societies might have declined rather than advanced. The fundamental point: technological ability is morally neutral. A rogue is a rogue, whether he is armed with a club or an AK-47; there are primitive barbarians and sophisticated barbarians.

The fallacy of thinking the primitive is superior because it is allegedly more natural is especially pernicious when it is used as it was by Mead: as a means to smuggle in a sophisticated and highly questionable theory about human nature. "Here is my theory. See, these natives exactly conform to my theory. Therefore, my theory must be correct."

We shall be able to see the fallacy more clearly in Mead's work if we set up a somewhat imaginary parallel with Hobbes, and allow him for a moment to be a traveling anthropologist. Hobbes argued that human beings are amoral by nature, and that in the state of nature they have the right to preserve themselves by any means possible, even by cannibalism. Imagine Hobbes on a working holiday. He boards a boat, sails off to find himself some anthropophagous Caribs, and writes *Coming of Age in the Caribbean*, which accurately describes a primitive society completely free from qualms about eating human beings. As they are more primitive, then they are closer to the state of nature; and as they are cannibals, they confirm that cannibalism is natural. Therefore, declares Hobbes, my theory must be true. Human beings are amoral by nature.

If we might put it in a more politically correct way, this fallacy is a form of intellectual and cultural colonialism pressed upon the poor natives against their will, a thinly disguised attempt at making them serve as the poster-primitives for yet another foreign agenda or cutting-edge revolutionary program.

What was Mead's agenda? Ostensibly, she traveled to Samoa to find out whether "rebellion against authority, philosophical perplexities, the flower of idealism, conflict and struggle" were "difficulties due to being an adolescent or to being adolescent in America."[1] Was all the turmoil of adolescence natural or merely a Western thing?

Of course this is a perfectly legitimate question, although it is certainly not one that a single short trip to Polynesia could settle. But even granting its legitimacy as a question, the famous opening paragraph of Chapter Two should raise a warning flag that Mead had packed a hidden agenda in her baggage:

> The life of the day begins at dawn, or if the moon has shown until daylight, the shouts of the young men may be heard before dawn from the hillside. Uneasy in the night, populous with ghosts, they shout lustily to one another as they hasten with their work. As the dawn begins to fall among the soft brown roofs and the slender palm trees stand out against a colourless, gleaming sea, lovers slip home from trysts beneath the palm trees or in the shadow of beached canoes, that the light may find each sleeper in his appointed place.[2]

This reads like the opening of a steamy romance novel, not a diligently conceived and executed book of anthropological research. To be more exact, Mead wrote it like a romance novel so that her hidden agenda would have the maximum popular impact (which it did). Her real goal was to convince the West that the rigors of Christian sexual morality were unnatural, and that its anxiety-producing inhibitions are something we'd all be happier without.

In other words, Mead was using the Samoans to push her own sexual schema, but that is not all she was pushing. As she makes clear in her finale, she was peddling an entirely new approach to education, "Education for Choice," one whose entire emphasis was to avoid any emphasis, and whose core belief was that there was no core belief:

> Education . . . instead of being a special pleading for one régime, a desperate attempt to form one particular habit of mind which will withstand all outside influences, must be a preparation for those very influences. . . . [The] child of the future must have an open mind. The home must cease to plead an ethical cause or a religious belief with smiles or frowns, caresses or threats. The children must be taught how to think, not what to think. And because old errors die slowly, they must be taught tolerance, just as to-day they are taught intolerance. They must be taught that many ways are open to them, no one sanctioned above its alternative, and that upon them and upon them alone lies the burden of choice. Unhampered by prejudices, unvexed by too early conditioning to any one standard, they must come clear-eyed to the choices which lie before them.[3]

Of course, an "open mind" to many different sexual ways, a "tolerance" of a multitude of sexual alternatives, was high on Mead's new educational agenda. So how did she squeeze this message out of the Samoans? She attempted to show that Samoan society was largely free of conflict—especially the "storm and stress [found] in American adolescents"—because the sources of conflict and anxiety embedded in our society were largely absent from Samoan society. If they were absent from Samoan society, then, Mead reasoned, they must not be natural.

For example, in Samoan society, there is very little conflict between parents and children because Samoan children are cared for indifferently by parents, aunts, uncles, cousins, and generally anyone older than they in the village. If a young girl does not like living under the same roof with her own parents, she just rolls up her mat and takes up residence with another relation. If a young boy finds his mother too demanding and his father uninviting, he simply decamps and recamps with a more pleasant set of kin. "No Samoan child . . . ever has to deal with a feeling of being trapped. There are always relatives to whom one can flee."[4]

Mead draws the conclusion that "it would be desirable [for us] to mitigate, at least in some slight measure, the strong role which parents play in children's lives,"[5] so that we might duplicate the weak role Samoan parents play in their children's lives. A happy effect of Samoans' not being tied to their parents is that they lack the "specialization of affection" (that is, intense, personal familial love) such as one finds in the modern West, with its "tiny, ingrown, biological family." In our "ingrown" family, there exist "strong ties between parents and children," but in the large and boisterous multi-generational, non-nuclear village life of the Samoans, "the home does not dominate and distort the life of the child" as it does in the West.[6] Children therefore form no special attachment to their own biological parents; as their affection is dispersed over an army of relatives, it is correspondingly weak in regard to any one person. Mead considers this a plus. Strong love makes for strong conflicts; weak love makes them few and light.

Of course, one of the most intense kinds of love is romantic love, which creates all kinds of emotional overloading, angst, and conflict—young star-crossed lovers vowing eternal allegiance unto death, tormented petitioners begging for the hand of a coquette, cuckolded spouses plotting murderous revenge. But here Mead finds again a "striking difference between Samoan society and our own," to wit, we find a "lack of the specialization of feeling, and particularly of sex feeling, among the Samoans."[7] "Romantic love as it occurs in our civilisation, inextricably bound up with ideas of monogamy, exclusiveness, jealousy, and undeviating fidelity does not occur in Samoa."[8] And why is that? Because the Samoans act pretty much like Rousseau's carefree lovers in the state of nature, engaging early and often in "free and easy experimentation."[9]

According to Mead, much of the energy of later adolescence is spent cavorting "under the palm trees."[10] Her anthropological focus was on the young women of Samoa, who, unlike their western counterparts, were completely free of sexual angst because they were completely free in regard to sex. Fala, Tolu, and Namu, ordinary representatives of Samoan feminine adolescence, all made "common rendezvous with their lovers and their liaisons were frequent and gay."[11] They bypassed the Western sexual storm and stress by making it all entirely casual, as Mead cheerfully reports:

> With the exception of a few cases...adolescence represented no period of crisis of stress, but was instead an orderly developing of a set of slowly maturing interests and activities. The girls' minds were perplexed by no conflicts, troubled by no philosophical queries, beset by no remote ambitions. To live as a girl with many lovers as long as possible and then to marry in one's own village, near one's own relatives and to have many children, these were uniform and satisfying ambitions.[12]

But the Samoan dedication to stress-free sex begins much earlier than adolescence, and the lack of "specialization" in regard to
sex leads them wandering merrily down many recreational
avenues. From very early on, children have "a vivid understanding of the nature of sex. Masturbation is an all but universal habit,
beginning at the age of six or seven," though it slackens a bit "with
the beginning of heterosexual activity" and for "grown boys and
girls casual homosexual practices also supplant it to a certain
extent."[13] Of course, homosexual encounters are not burdened by
anxiety either:

> These casual homosexual relations between girls never assumed
> any long-term importance. On the part of growing girls or
> women who were working together they were regarded as a
> pleasant and natural diversion, just tinged with the salacious.
> Where heterosexual relationships were so casual, so shallowly
> channeled, there was no pattern into which homosexual rela-
> tionships could fall.[14]

Whereas we in the West get all worked up about both heterosexuality and homosexuality, the Samoans bypass our entire set of
cultural anxieties and antagonisms by regarding all sex as merely
play. We are narrow-minded about sex; they are entirely open-
minded. We spend our time arguing in divorce courts, untying the
knots of our neuroses on analysts' couches, and battling over where
to draw acceptable lines regarding sexual conduct. Samoans spend
their time as Rousseau's bonobos, casually scratching whatever
itches. The casual nature of their heterosexuality keeps them from
getting uptight about homosexuality like us high-collared puritan-
ical types in the West.

The general preoccupation with sex, the attitude that minor sex activities, suggestive dancing, stimulating and salacious conversation, salacious songs and definitely motivated tussling are all acceptable and attractive diversions, is mainly responsible for the native attitude towards homosexual practices. They are simply *play*, neither frowned upon nor given much consideration. As heterosexual relations are given significance not by love and tremendous fixation upon the individual, the only forces which can make a homosexual relationship lasting and important, but by children and the place of marriage in the economic and social structure of the village, it is easy to understand why very prevalent homosexual practices have no more important or striking results. The recognition and use in heterosexual relations of all the secondary variations of sex activity which loom as primary in homosexual relations are instrumental also in minimizing their importance.[15]

The way to get over sexual hang-ups, then, is sexual saturation of the culture. If sex is entirely indiscriminate, and the moral cords that entangle us have all been cut, then we'll recover our natural, anxiety-free existence—and not just before marriage. Repeating Rousseau's moral inversion, Mead implies that it is the foolish desire for fidelity that creates marital conflict; the unnatural bonds of lifelong monogamy create lifelong misery. Loosen the bonds and the load is lightened.

If . . . a wife really tires of her husband, or a husband of his wife, divorce is a simple and informal matter, the non-resident simply going home to his or her family, and the relationship is said to have "passed away." It is a very brittle monogamy, often trespassed and more often broken entirely. But many adulteries

occur... which hardly threaten the continuity of established rela-
tionships. The claim that a woman has on her family's land ren-
ders her as independent as her husband, and so there are no
marriages of any duration in which either person is actively
unhappy. A tiny flare-up and a woman goes home to her people; if her husband does not care to conciliate her, each seeks
another mate.[16]

So, you see, the problem with Westerners is that by "recognizing only one narrow form of sex activity," we channel our libido
far too early into far too restricted a conduit, which must eventually "result in unsatisfactory marriages."[17] If we just bypassed the
restrictions from the beginning and let the sexual urges flow where
they will, then by the time of marriage we could be as casual and
carefree as the Samoans. The best way to a no-fault divorce is rid-
ding ourselves of the burdensome and unnatural notion of faults.
In fact, the whole notion that there are moral faults in regard to
sexuality is—as Freud would have it—the cause of our deep neurotic malaise. Not so for the Samoans. They teach us that the very
notion of sexual perversion is a perversion:

By discounting our category of perversion, as applied to practice,
and reserving it for the occasional psychic pervert, they legislate
a whole field of neurotic possibility out of existence. Onanism,
homosexuality, statistically unusual forms of heterosexual activity, are neither banned nor institutionalised. The wider range
which these practices give prevents the development of obses-
sions of guilt which are so frequent a cause of maladjustment
among us. The more varied practices permitted heterosexually
preserve any individual from being penalised for special condi-
tioning. This acceptance of a wider range as "normal" provides
a cultural atmosphere in which frigidity and psychic impotence

do not occur and in which a satisfactory sex adjustment in marriage can always be established. The acceptance of such an attitude without in any way accepting promiscuity would go a long
way towards solving many marital impasses and emptying our
park benches and our houses of prostitution.[18]

Without in any way accepting promiscuity? If this is normal,
what could possibly count as being promiscuous? However that
may be, Mead makes clear that the casual attitude toward sex is
just part of the Samoan's don't-worry-be-happy attitude about
everything. What "makes growing up so easy, so simple a matter,
is the general casualness of the whole society" toward everything
in heaven and on earth:

> For Samoa is a place where no one plays for very high stakes,
> no one pays very heavy prices, no one suffers for his convictions
> or fights to the death for special ends. Disagreements between
> parent and child are settled by the child's moving across the
> street, between a man and his village by the man's removal to
> the next village, between a husband and his wife's seducer by a
> few fine [woven] mats [given as gifts]. Neither poverty nor great
> disasters threaten the people to make them hold their lives
> dearly and tremble for continued existence. No implacable
> gods, swift to anger and strong to punish, disturb the even tenor
> of their days.[19]

One might well wonder about the implacability of the gods on
Samoa, given that it had been mission territory for Christians
since the mid-nineteenth century. Mead's answer—which, of
course, she wished to be instructive for the Christian West—was
that Samoans' wore their Christianity like their native garb, very
lightly and easily cast aside when suitable occasions presented

themselves. As Mead would have it, "the only dissenters" in regard to the Samoan casual attitude toward sexual mores "are the missionaries who dissent so vainly that their protests are unimportant."[20] The "moral premium on chastity" introduced by the missionaries was met "with reverent but complete skepticism and the concept of celibacy is absolutely meaningless to them."[21] The "Missionary influence... has failed to give the native a conviction of Sin," even though it has "provided him with a list of sins."[22] The result is that on Samoa, "the whole religious setting is one of formalism [i.e., going through the motions but without deep convictions], of compromise, of acceptance of half-measure. The great number of native pastors with their peculiar interpretations of Christian teaching have made it impossible to establish the rigour of western Protestantism with its inseparable association of sex offences and an individual consciousness of sin."[23] That's all to the good, as a liberal and pliable version of Christianity means that religion produces very little anxiety. Another plus and another lesson for the neurosis-producing ecclesiastics on our side of the Pacific.

What, then, is Mead's take-home lesson? We in the West "live in a period of transition."[24] Unlike the Samoans, who live in a stable but promiscuous society, Westerners are in a state of flux, deluged by multiple standards, multiple ways of life, multiple notions of religion, multiple ideas about sexuality. Our stress, especially the stress of adolescence, is likewise multiplied. The Samoans are carefree because they have so little to restrict their sexuality, they are not bound tightly by parental bonds, they look forward to living an easy life in a simple culture that doesn't afflict them with endless, competing choices about what to do with their lives. Americans are harried by conflict and choice because "progress" has opened up a morass of competing worldviews. What to do?

Obviously, we cannot return to native simplicity, but we can import the Samoan casualness about all things sexual into our culture and let the steam out of stress by setting a cultural premium on individual choice and complete tolerance. Our problem is that we are faced with "many standards but we still believe that only one standard can be the right one." No wonder we're stressed out. We must embrace the notion that standards are like a plethora of goods for the picking at a bazaar—to each his own, and the more bizarre the better. Let there be only one standard: that no one interfere with another's standards. There can be no right because there can be no wrong, and no wrong because no one can be definitively right.

Mead's battle cry, then, is that we need to march forward and create a new era, "when no one group claims ethical sanction for its customs, and each group welcomes to its midst only those who are temporarily fitted for membership." Then, Mead beams, "we shall have realised the high point of individual choice and universal toleration which a heterogeneous culture and a heterogeneous culture alone can attain."[25]

This should all sound so familiar that to comment on its becoming the platform for twentieth-century liberalism's cultural revolutions would be superfluous. Ditto Mead's notion that sexual restrictions, rather than saving us from devilry and self-destruction, cause unhealthy neurotic implosion.

Something must be said about Mead's own work as scientific propaganda. "Science," like patriotism, can be the last (and sometimes first) refuge of scoundrels. In 1983 anthropologist Derek Freeman charged Mead (who had died about five years earlier a hallowed cultural-intellectual icon), with entirely misrepresenting the Samoans. "The main conclusions of *Coming of Age in Samoa*," he argued, "are, in reality, the figments of an anthropological myth which is deeply at variance with the facts of Samoan ethnography and history."[26] As it turns out, argued Freeman, the Samoans were far more concerned with chastity, and hence far less sexually promiscuous, than Westerners of the time. Freeman's point was pointed: Mead imposed her own agenda upon the Samoans.

Freeman's case is certainly plausible. Whatever the Samoans were doing, Mead herself acted much like her allegedly free-wheeling natives, leading one to believe that her anthropology was a thinly disguised autobiography she was waiting to act out. She was married when she sailed to Samoa, but ditched her first husband for a man she met on the journey back home. The second was soon traded for a third, and finally her third marriage was casually cast aside. The whole time she was carrying on with her lesbian lover, Ruth Benedict. As she later stated quite frankly, "rigid heterosexuality is a perversion of nature."[27] In her ideal society, she confided, people would be homosexual when young, then switch to some heterosexuality during the breeding years, then switch back again.[28] Was Mead painting the Samoans with her own colors?

Freeman's criticism caused a sensation, and a rhetorical battle has raged ever since. Some have questioned Freeman's analysis of Samoan culture, and hence his criticisms of Mead, whose status as a liberal cultural icon has been damaged but not overthrown. Meanwhile, anthropologist Martin Orans has leveled an entirely different but equally damning charge at Mead. According to Orans, Freeman didn't really prove that Mead was mistaken about the Samoans; her methods were so shoddy that her conclusions were not even substantiated well enough to be wrong. Hence the title of his book, *Not Even Wrong: Margaret Mead, Derek Freeman, and the Samoans.* The real question is: how did Mead's *Coming of Age in Samoa*—which Orans shows to be riddled with "extensive method-

ological faults" and plagued by a "paucity or absence of support-
ing data for her argument"[29]—become so influential? More to the
point, "How could anthropologists and other eminent scholars
have largely ignored such blatant defects? How could generations
of university professors have included *CA* [*Coming of Age in Samoa*]
as required reading for students? How could such a flawed work
have served as a stepping-stone to fame?"[30]

Orans says reason number one is "ideological." "We wanted
Mead's findings to be correct. We believed that a more permissive
sexual code would be of benefit to us all. More important, her findings were a coup for the proponents of the importance of culture
vis-à-vis biology. This perspective supported solving human problems by social change, whereas the emphasis on biology insisted
that our problems were rooted in human nature and therefore
ineradicable." The message that with sexual permissiveness and
social re-engineering we could have a lot more fun and completely
eliminate society's problems as well had a ready audience in the
early twentieth century (and still does today).

Reason number two is rooted in the discipline of cultural
anthropology itself—or perhaps, the lack of discipline. According
to Orans, himself a practicing anthropologist, "From its inception,
its practice has often been profoundly unscientific and positively
cavalier in its willingness to accept generalizations without empirical substantiation."[31] Anthropology was thus the perfect scientific
cover for cultural analysis that was no more scientific than the state
of nature imagined by Hobbes and Rousseau.

The desire that something be true, rather than the desire for
truth itself, may well be the root of all evil. It is certainly the origin
of all ideology, and ideology was the source of much of the evil in
the past century.

What is ideology? We live in such an ideological age that it's hard for us to distinguish good thinking from bad. The crucial distinction is that ideology is not philosophy. Philosophy is the love of wisdom, the love of what is real, whether we happen to like it or not. It is the desire for truth, and the continual humility to remold our desires to fit reality. Ideology comes at truth from the opposite direction, molding truth to what we happen to desire. Because it has no compunction about refashioning truth to fit our desires, it has no hesitation, in the hands of someone like Mead, in refashioning reality according to our cravings. Pseudo-science is thus the handmaid to ideology. Politics is its hammer.

Mead provides a classic example of the power of ideology in creating and perpetrating pseudo-science. As Orans makes clear, the desire to create a sexual revolution made all too many highly intelligent scientists (who should have known better) accept and exalt Mead's work even though, by the accepted canons of science, it had more holes than cloth in the fabric of the argument. But they wanted it to be true. "Had the book been similarly unscientific but with an opposite ideology," remarks Orans candidly, "we no doubt would have ripped it apart for its scientific failings."[32]

Of course, Mead isn't the only one guilty of successfully peddling pseudo-science. Marx and Engels thought themselves eminently scientific, as did Darwin, Freud, Hitler, and Sanger. And when we take up Kinsey, we'll see sexual perversion parading as science in the borrowed austerity of a lab coat. But we can't just blame these execrable authors. Bad books screw up the world only if they are consumed eagerly by those who are hungry to hear their messages: that it would be good to eliminate the "unfit" rather than caring for them charitably; that all evil is caused by one class or race and can be eliminated by the elimination of those people; that we can become geniuses by engaging in sexual bacchanalia; and that easy sex, easy divorce, easy parents, easy standards, and easy religion will cure all that ails us.

In each of these cases, it is the cure that kills.

CHAPTER FOURTEEN

Sexual Behavior in the Human Male (1948)

Alfred Kinsey (1894–1956)

AS THE READER WILL SEE, WE HAVE NO QUOTATION FROM ALFRED Kinsey's *Sexual Behavior in the Human Male* to start off the chapter. Nor will any quotes be found within the chapter itself. There is a very simple—and very telling—reason for this. The Kinsey Institute for Research in Sex, Gender, and Reproduction will not allow me to quote anything. This is both aggravating and revealing.

It is aggravating because I assumed (according to the usual custom with publishers and copyright holders), that I would be granted permission, so I had written the chapter some months before publication of my book. I filled it with direct quotes from Kinsey's *Sexual Behavior* for the obvious reason that an author ought to be judged by his own words.

That brings us to the revealing part. The Kinsey Institute refused me permission to quote from *Sexual Behavior in the Human Male.*

Evidently, the Institute does not want its namesake to be judged by his own words. As with Margaret Sanger, Kinsey's own words are a public embarrassment. To be blunt, the Kinsey Institute is censoring its own man (and little wonder, given the quotes I had lined up).

Back to the aggravating part. As a result, I've had to rewrite the entire chapter at the last minute. But since I try to be a scrupulous scholar, you will see that I footnote everything very exactly, so that you, the reader, may skirt the Kinsey Institute's blackout of *Sexual Behavior in the Human Male.*

So, here we go with the (somewhat) censored, secondhand *report* of what Kinsey said. In Kinsey's work, many of the worst streams we've seen in previous books flow together into one reeking pool: the belief that our natural state is one of amoral sexual extravaganza; the evolutionary reduction of human beings to the level of animals; the adept use of science to mask propaganda; the attack on the Judeo-Christian understanding of male, female, marriage, and family. Even more than Rousseau or Mead, Kinsey's revolution was intensely personal, a revolution rooted in his own epic sexual perversity. He represents, in sterling coin, the evil that results from attempting to change the world to match one's character, rather than changing oneself to match the deep moral order written into human nature.

While Kinsey's book was by no means the first manifesto of modernity's sexual uprising, it was certainly the book that broke the dam. Released in 1948, it washed away every moral boundary of sexuality with a torrent of charts, graphs, and technical lingo. Kinsey's careful posturing in lab coats, his dour glare as he churned out data to the naysayers, his aura of disinterested objectivity—all were calculated to one effect: to ram through the sexual revolution as just another aspect of the scientific revolution.

It was not until the release of James Jones's biography of Kinsey in 1997 that the lab coat and scientific screen were ripped away to reveal the seething fleshpots of Kinsey's private life. If his secret sexual saturnalia had seen the light of day fifty years earlier, Kinsey's book would have been revealed as what it really was: a thickly disguised attempt to force the world to accept his own unnatural sexuality as natural. But, alas, by the time Jones's *Alfred C. Kinsey: A Public/Private Life* came out, the revolution was over, and Kinsey had won.

Even without the full light of day shining on Kinsey's private darkness, we should have known better. His *Sexual Behavior in the Human Male* (or, for short, the *Kinsey Report*) is a scientific sham that could have been exposed upon its first release. In fact, many of its obvious defects were pointed out at the time. But the sad truth is that, as with Mead's *Coming of Age in Samoa*, too many people were eager to hear the sexual sermon preached by Kinsey, and the pseudo-scientific trappings simply helped to ease their consciences.

Kinsey asserted, right at the beginning, that there was nothing that had done more to obstruct the free investigation of sex than the nearly universal acceptance—even among scientists—that some kinds of behavior were normal, and some abnormal. The cause of the obstruction? The obvious connection between normal and abnormal, and right and wrong. Kinsey views this connection as an unwelcome incursion of morality into the pure world of science, and assures the reader that he has slammed the door in morality's face. We are only reporting on what men do, not on what they *should* do, Kinsey tells us; just reporting the facts about the sexual behavior of the American male as we find him, *whatever* he does.[1]

That's Kinsey's entire strategy in the original nutshell. Instead of asking the old-fashioned question "How should we act?" Kinsey asks the seemingly scientific question "How do we really act?" Science, he claims, deals with the "is," not the "ought." When we find out how men actually act, then we will finally have a trustworthy account of sexual behavior in the human male.

What could be wrong with that? As I mentioned before, I was purified of my romantic notions of roosters and hens by raising them in our backyard. Before experiencing how roosters actually act, my vision of a "normal" rooster was fashioned by Walt Disney's generally rose-colored view of animals. All of us were quite scandalized to find out that real roosters have not a pin-feather of chivalry. The rooster's idea of romance is to savagely and regularly leap upon the ladies and rip their back feathers out with his beak while rudely having his way. After several weeks of listening to the hens' pain-filled shrieks, we moved the roosters into our freezer. Reality was the cure for our romantic notions. The "is" of roosters was too much to bear, but we had given up any notion of them changing their ways to what they "ought" to be. I have since thought of penning a revealing *Sexual Behavior in the Inhumane Rooster.*

So what could be wrong with Kinsey's approach? After all, science should serve up the hard facts, however hard they may be to swallow. The problem with Kinsey's approach—one of the problems—is precisely his denial of the "ought" for a particular view of the "is." This approach has its roots in the Darwinian confusion of animals with human beings, but can also trace its ancestry back to the illustrious Machiavelli.

As to the first rotten root, Kinsey was a passionate Darwinist, earning his Ph.D. from Harvard University in entomology and becoming a world-class expert on the gall wasp. Kinsey saw infinite and continual variation in nature as an essential evolutionary fact, not just of gall wasps, but even more important, of human beings and their endless sexual variations. There were no boundaries in nature: one species blended into another just as seamlessly as one human sexual proclivity shaded into another, all without a trace of sharp boundary. Thus, the endless possible sexual variations and expressions we find in human males are no more perverse or immoral than the endless variations in form found among successive generations of gall wasps discovered by the entomologist. Variety is the spice of evolution and sex. Whatever happens, it must be natural.

Reaching beyond Darwin to Machiavelli, we see on a deeper level a kind of Machiavellian assertion that the world should be defined by what most people actually do, rather than by some kind of pie-in-the-sky notion of what they should do. Machiavelli urged that most actual princes lie, cheat, steal, and kill when it suits their purposes, and that makes them much more effective princes. This means, in a sense, that princes should act like animals: creatures that have no moral boundaries. Accordingly, Machiavelli counsels princes that they should learn to act like the lion in its savagery and the fox in its trickery, and both without a care as to Judeo-Christian notions of what is right or wrong.

Kinsey wrote that most people satisfy their sexual urges in a number of ways, and (as he attempts to show) that makes them all the happier and more natural. They ignore moral boundaries and do whatever tickles their fancies. Kinsey counsels his readers that as animals they should feel free to act like any other animal in satisfying their sexual urges, and precisely because they are only animals, they can discard the Judeo-Christian notions of right and wrong.

As Kinsey is intent on treating us like beasts, it is perhaps all too appropriate to illustrate his approach by examining his discussion of bestiality. He begins his discussion in a typically patronizing way, noting that many people ignorantly assume that two mating animals should actually be from the same species. Of course, that is usually the case, admits Kinsey, but such childlike trust that what happens for the most part is universal is, well, merely childish—especially when it assumes that there is some kind of universal moral reason why only animals from the same species should mate. If people only knew, chides Kinsey, how many exceptions there are to the rule! The equivalent of bestiality among animals—animals of one species trying to mate with animals of another species—is all too common of an exception to ignore.[2] So, if you are so childishly foolish as to think bestiality beastly, then you just don't know how often it actually occurs among the beasts themselves. According to Kinsey, recent scientists have uncovered myriad instances of such interspecific matings, even among the higher animals.[3]

Seeing that all the birds and bees do it, and nearly every creature up each branch of the evolutionary tree does it, then the true scientist begins to suspect that there's a lot more exceptions than most have been willing to admit and the exceptions call into question some hallowed sexual rules.[4]

And so, just what exactly does that mean for us? Since we now know how common such things are in the animal kingdom—a kingdom in which we are fellow subjects and citizens—it seems quite odd that we would find bestiality so . . . creepy. Especially, adds Kinsey, since most of us have not *had the experience of bestiality ourselves* (shades of Mill's dilemma: only those who have delved into bestiality can judge whether it is good or bad).[5] Such abhorrence is obviously unscientific and unhistorical. Certainly human-animal sexual contact has taken place since the dawn of human history, Kinsey informs the reader, and we find it in all contemporary cultures even today—including our own. And the reason is simple, sexual physics: the sexual forces that bring individuals of the same species together, also bring individuals of different species together.[6]

As for the data in regard to our own culture, Kinsey cheerfully reports that among boys raised down on the farm, about 17 percent have had sex with animals before adolescence. If we count up all sexual contacts, the number climbs to just about half. And since we can expect folks to hide such socially unacceptable facts, we may feel free to double those numbers. Just think, muses Kinsey, how many people would be having sex with animals if it were not frowned upon by our society![7]

The point is simple for Kinsey. Given the frequency of bestiality throughout the animal kingdom and in our own farmyards, there is no scientific reason for thinking it immoral. The sole reason for condemning it comes from ignorance and prejudice on the part of the non–bestially inclined.[8] As for those who may have indulged and now feel guilty, this is all very good news, for informed psychologists can reassure them that such activity is just a normal part of being an animal.[9]

That's Kinsey's strategy in action. There are no such things as sexual deviations. If something happens sexually, it must be part of the natural spectrum; if it is part of the natural spectrum, it cannot be considered either abnormal or unnatural, even if it is relatively uncommon; but as it turns out to be so much more common than anyone suspected, then it really must be quite normal and hence quite natural.

Since bestiality is the last subject treated in *Sexual Behavior in the Human Male*, the above reasoning flows right into his crashing conclusion. There is no good or bad, right or wrong, normal or abnormal way to express one's sexuality. It's all natural, every bit of it. While the six types of sexual activity covered in *Sexual Behavior* (masturbation, spontaneous nocturnal emissions, petting, heterosexual intercourse, homosexual contacts, and animal contacts), may *seem* to fall into categories as distant as as right and wrong, licit and illicit, normal and abnormal, acceptable and unacceptable, in fact they are all just different responses to the same sexual mechanisms.[10]

Here we have an interesting legacy of Descartes, who gave us the dualist self, a spirit trapped in a machine. When the spirit dropped out and full-blown mechanism was accepted, the path was cleared for the expression of human sexuality as a merely mechanical response, with no more moral dimension to it than an alarm clock going off.

We also find the patrimony of Rousseau and his pre-moral paradise. If we had no artificial restrictions on our sexuality, muses Kinsey, if we had never been burdened by notions of right and wrong, normal or abnormal, but had been allowed to wander wherever our lust led us in a pre-moral Rousseau's garden, things would have been *much* different. If there were no artificially restrictive notions of sexual morality, individuals would have been mechanically conditions to a variety of sexual activities—even and especially ones they now find revolting. There simply is no such thing as innate sexual perversity.[11] That "conclusion" is, as we'll soon see, good news for Kinsey who longed for science to stamp his personal perversities with approval.

Before examining Kinsey's own life, we need to bring up the obvious problems with Kinsey's approach. To declare that something is natural because it happens both among animals and among human beings is, to say the least, a dicey way to proceed. The chickens in my own backyard will provide an illustration. When one of the hens gets hurt or sick, the other hens will soon enough begin to peck at it, and if we don't isolate the beleaguered hen, she'll be pecked to death in short order. And then it may well turn into cannibalism time (as it does when a baby chick dies). Should we then declare such behavior natural for human beings?

Speaking of enjoying a family meal, as is well known, the female praying mantis, black widow, and several other such critters resort to cannibalism after mating. From insects right up to lions and chimps, cannibalism happens all the time, with (one suspects) as much or more frequency as "interspecific matings."

Shall we then say the following, in a Kinseyesque manner? "To many persons it will seem almost a truism that individuals of the same species should not eat each other. This is so often true, from one end of the animal kingdom to the other, that exceptions to the rule seem especially worthy of note. Of course, children believe that conformity to the rule should be universal, any departure from the rule being immoral. This immorality may seem particularly gross to an individual who is unaware of the frequency with which exceptions to the *supposed* rule actually occur." What if we offered the following rhetorical rumination? "It certainly is interesting to note the degree of horror with which cannibalism is viewed by most persons who have not eaten another human being, but they are merely being provincial and prejudiced." Or, if from historical documents and police records, we found that cannibalism has occurred down through the ages and right up to our own age, what should we say about it? "It is certain that cannibalism has been known since the dawn of history, and even found among all people of today—even in our own culture. We should not be surprised—the record simply substantiates our present scientific understanding that the forces which bring individuals to eat members of other species may sometimes bring individuals to eat members of their own species." These are all very slightly modified quotes from Kinsey, the only difference being the substitution of "cannibalism" for "bestiality."

And as for the poor cannibals themselves, happily psychologists can assure them that cannibalism is "biologically and psychologically part of the normal mammalian picture."

The point is obvious, one should hope, and it could be made with all manner of activities that do in fact occur among animals and among human beings: rape, murder, incest, and pedophilia. In each case, applying Kinsey's supposedly scientific method would produce the same result. Each and every one might seem to fall into the dark side of the categories of right and wrong, licit and illicit, normal and abnormal, acceptable and unacceptable, but as they all in fact do occur, they must be considered natural.

That would be the end result if Kinsey's approach really were "scientific" and, as he promised, entirely devoid of moral intrusions. In short, Kinsey's method leads to the madness of Hobbes's amoral state of nature, where right and wrong have no place.

Of course, Kinsey didn't want to loosen all the moral chains, only the sexual ones. He was therefore willing to declare a Hobbesian sexual state of nature (one far more brutal and bestial than Rousseau's relatively tame sexual Eden), even while avoiding the obvious implications we've drawn out.

Why? Because Kinsey's own sexual perversities were so astounding that the only way to escape the unnaturalness of his activities was to declare them to be natural, to say that there was no sexual good or evil. In short, Kinsey's private life was a Hobbesian sexual state of nature.

Without going into too much detail, it is important to know that Kinsey was a devoted homosexual sado-masochist who masturbated while ramming large objects (like toothbrushes, bristle-end first) into his urethra and simultaneously strangling his testicles with a rope. He had sex with all his male colleagues quite frequently, and they traded wives as well. He also regularly commandeered his own wife,

Clara, for all manner of deviance for the cameras at the Institute for Sex Research at Indiana University. As James Jones's biography makes painfully clear, Kinsey was a sexually twisted man, and the later Kinsey-friendly biography by Jonathan Gathorne-Hardy, *Kinsey: Sex the Measure of All Things*, corroborates the sordid picture even while attempting to cast Kinsey in a positive light. (A single astounding example. In regard to the toothbrush incident and all the other interesting instruments Kinsey employed, Gathorne-Hardy says, "How should we view Kinsey's experiments? As usual, we can admire his courage."[12]) Gathorne-Hardy was, by the way, the consultant for the Hollywood whitewash *Kinsey*, starring Liam Neeson.

Kinsey's sexual revolution was a very personal thing, then. In fact, it was simply Kinsey writ large in diagrams, charts, and reams of data. All were marshaled to establish that Kinsey was the natural man, man as he would be if his sexuality had never been chained by unnatural moral shackles.

Kinsey's revolutionary program was primarily concerned with liberating homosexuality, and the first step in breaking down the moral boundary against homosexuality was to change the focus of the discussion. Kinsey claimed that it would encourage clearer thinking on these matters if people were not characterized as either heterosexual or homosexual. Rather, one should tally up the kind of sexual experiences they've had, either heterosexual or homosexual.[13] If we do it this way, we find out that one out of every three men we meet walking down the street has had some kind of homosexual experience in the time from the beginning of adolescence to old age.[14] Kinsey's approach allowed moral black and white to be smeared into a broad gray swath with no sharp edges. Sharp moral categories are fictions of the human mind.[15]

While Kinsey's strategy was quite effective, it was not quite scientific. To begin with, there was the little problem of where he got the data. The interview pool that yielded the conclusion that one in three men on the street had "homosexual experience" failed to mention that a large percentage of the interviewees were men *of* the street: several hundred of them were male prostitutes. Many who were not plying their trade on the streets were behind bars: 25 percent of the pool were sex offenders or had been in prison for other reasons. Moreover, Kinsey's interviewers purposely sought out the "rarer" types of imprisoned sex offenders in order to create the impression that deviancy was normal.[16] When Kinsey ventured beyond these sordid circles, he scouted out what best suited his purposes, seeking interviewees from homosexual networks. As Jones points out, this habit of "targeting homosexuals" from very early on in his gathering of data "would skew his sample in the years ahead."[17] Finally, even though Kinsey was warned, he took no account of "volunteer bias." The kind of person likely to volunteer to have his sexual history taken is the kind of person most likely to be sexually deviant.

There is also the problem of how Kinsey presented the data. Even if the one-in-three statistic were not highly inflated, it included both frantically active, lifelong homosexuals and those who had only one fleeting homosexual experience in boyhood. That is the equivalent of saying that more than one-third of the men you meet are thieves, when what you mean is that a very few men are actually thieves and a very large number of boys once stole a pack of gum.

Using such rigging and rolling of data, Kinsey was able to outfit a raft of statistics that made homosexuality nearly as common as heterosexuality. Only a mere 50 percent of the population is exclusively heterosexual through its adult life, and only 4 percent are exclusively homosexual. Well, then, that means that almost half of all the men engage in both heterosexual and homosexual acts![18]

Homosexuality is not, then, some kind of a peculiar sexual deviation; it is just one more normal sexual expression. If our culture were not so artificially restrictive, the percentage of the ambisextrous would be much higher, perhaps closer to 100 percent. The fact that homosexuality was widespread in other cultures, would seem to prove that, if such artificial restrictions were removed, then we'd revert to our natural state of sexual free-for-all.[19]

In other words, the Judeo-Christian prohibition of homosexuality is artificial and hence unnatural. Since it forms the basis of our Anglo-American culture, then Judaism and Christianity are unnatural. It should not surprise us that Kinsey was a vehement atheist. But ancient Greece was also known for its pedophilia. If we followed Kinsey's reasoning, then we would be affirming pedophilia as likewise natural, just one more way that individuals can respond erotically. Surely Kinsey couldn't mean that?

Indeed. It is a wonder that Kinsey wasn't arrested after the publication of his infamous *Report*, as not a few pages are dedicated to the affirmation of pre-adolescent sexuality, using the data gathered from the histories of men who had sexual contacts with younger boys.[20] Kinsey cheerfully tabulates the orgasm statistics of babies as young as four or five months and announces that the most remarkable aspect of the pre-adolescent population is its capacity to achieve repeated orgasms in astonishingly limited periods of time—why, nearly a third of the 182 boys "studied" was able to have five or more sexual climaxes in rapid succession.[21] Kinsey then conjectures wistfully that, if such unnatural moral restrictions against pedophilia were dropped, the rapid orgasm rates of pre-adolescents could be boosted to over fifty percent![22] Of course, being good scientists, we recognize that the naturalness of pedophilia is confirmed by reports of its occurrence among other mammals.[23]

Kinsey had no anxiety about using data collected by child molesters because he believed that the very notion of "molesting"—a negative term—was a holdover from religious hang-ups. Science was the cure for such religio-moral obscurantism. A good Darwinian approach, a scientific approach, puts pre-adolescent sexuality in the proper context, as just one more way to "express" ourselves.

One can barely stand to read the sections of Kinsey's *Sexual Behavior in the Human Male* on the repeated raping of babies and small children. What makes it so thoroughly nauseating is the high-sounding pretence to scientific objectivity. It all appears hauntingly like the Nazi researchers' detached, objective accounts of their experiments on living victims. Both, no doubt, yielded real data, and in both we are faced with a science twisted to purposes that destroy the humanity of victim and perpetrator, all in the name of human progress.

So there we have Kinsey. Of course, he undermined any notion that pre-marital sex and adultery were wrong using the very same kind of reasoning. Since it all appeared so scientific, and we wanted to hear it, Kinsey's pseudo-science became foundational for the sexual revolution, used both in courts and classrooms to push a limitless sexual revolution that began in the 1960s and through which we are still living. This revolution will not be over until it has overthrown all sexual boundaries, which means that it will not be complete until it extinguishes all opposition, the greatest of which is Christianity. Once again, we see atheism at the root of rebellion.

Part III
Dishonorable Mention

CHAPTER FIFTEEN

The Feminine Mystique (1963)

*"As she made the beds, shopped for groceries,
matched slipcover material, ate peanut butter sandwiches
with her children, chauffeured Cub Scouts and Brownies,
lay beside her husband at night—she was afraid to ask even
of herself the silent question—'Is this all?'"*

Betty Friedan (1921–2006)

I END WITH A CONSIDERATION OF BETTY FRIEDAN'S *THE FEMININE Mystique*, not because we need a "token" female (we already have Margaret Sanger and Margaret Mead; bad books are an equal opportunity employer), but because we need a token of feminism, a movement that left its own distinct historical mark even while it shared in many of the assumptions we've already seen.

Betty Friedan is credited with launching the second wave of feminism—though some of the original feminists (like Susan B. Anthony), had they lived to see her, might have repudiated her. As with Mead and Kinsey, Friedan's private life makes for an illuminating gloss upon her writings, especially her most famous, *The Feminine Mystique*. Once again, we see autobiography masquerading as science—and we can see how much the second wave of feminism was defined by Friedan's personality and personal conflicts.

She was born in Peoria, Illinois, Bettye (not Betty originally) Naomi Goldstein, the daughter of Harry Goldstein, a jeweler, and his domineering and bitter but beautiful young wife, Miriam Horwitz Goldstein. Both parents were Jewish immigrants, and the upper-middle-class Goldstein family suffered its share of callous snubbing. From her father, Bettye inherited her atheism. From her mother, she inherited a violent temper. Her mother's stunning beauty went entirely to Bettye's sister Amy. As even her most sympathetic biographers note, Bettye was quite homely (which her mother never let her forget), and this consciousness of her unattractiveness coupled with her aching desire for romance seared her soul deeply from early childhood.

But just as scarring was her hot-tempered mother, all sweetness to those outside and a witch to her own family. She looked down on her husband, considering herself too high-society for him, and Bettye's prominent nose, bequeathed by her father, increased her hostility toward Bettye. The Goldstein house was filled with rancor as Miriam spent far beyond Harry's means to properly adorn her elevated self-image (even when the Great Depression hit the jeweler's business hard), and continually berated Bettye.

To add a particularly important bitterness to an already harsh marital stew, Harry had insisted Miriam quit her job writing for the society pages and devote herself to being a housewife. By her own admission, Bettye would associate her mother's constant rage and the consequent deep unhappiness of the Goldstein home with her mother's bitterness at having to give up socialite journalism. Finding a cure for this childhood misery is the hidden autobiographical substrate of *The Feminine Mystique*.

The Feminine Mystique is a very long book, much longer than it needs to be for its quite simple message: women who are only wives and mothers are secretly or openly miserable because they cannot venture outside the home and cheerfully maximize their potential as human beings in meaningful work, just as men do. Boiled down to the bones, the flaws of *The Feminine Mystique* become apparent. Friedan seems to assume that men working outside the home are happily fulfilling their deepest human longings in "meaningful" work as journalists, college professors, advertising executives, airplane pilots, and doctors, rather than engaging in the actual drudgery, the real bone-grinding and mind-numbing toil, which fills the days of almost all actual working men, and which finds them wearily sapped of strength at the end of the day. It assumes a kind of glamour—mystique, we might dare call it—to working outside the home that real experience in the actual work that most men do in ditches, factories, welding shops, and even banks and accounting firms, would cure.

This abstractness from actual conditions mars much of Friedan's analysis. Before she published *The Feminine Mystique*, Friedan had spent years in Marxist-inspired agitation on behalf of mistreated lower-class workers—and the abstractness of her analysis is fundamentally Marxist.

But we are getting ahead of ourselves. At this juncture, we need to make one fairly simple assertion about Friedan. Friedan romanticized working outside the home and demonized the role of housewife. She did so on the basis not only of her mother's volcanic discontent at staying home, but also of her own. She assumed, as cold fact, that all women suffered the same restless dissatisfaction as her mother and herself.

Such is clear from the opening chapters of *The Feminine Mystique*, in which Friedan attempts to demonstrate that, despite their seeming contentment and the unsettling trend (unsettling to Friedan, at least) of women marrying enthusiastically and early, housewives were sorely afflicted with "the problem that has no name":

The problem lay buried, unspoken, for many years in the minds of American women. It was a strange stirring, a sense of dissatisfaction, a yearning that women suffered in the middle of the twentieth century in the United States. Each suburban wife struggled with it alone. As she made the beds, shopped for groceries, matched slipcover material, ate peanut butter sandwiches with her children, chauffeured Cub Scouts and Brownies, lay beside her husband at night—she was afraid to ask even of herself the silent question—"Is this all?"[1]

These heart-rent housewives, claimed Friedan, had been sold a bill of goods designed to keep them in shackles—the "feminine mystique," the notion that "they could desire no greater destiny than to glory in their own femininity," and claim "Occupation: Housewife" as the sum of their status. But according to Friedan, the happy façade was rapidly peeling away. As women's magazines and the latest psychological research demonstrated, the suburban housewife was a cauldron of neurotic discontent boiling over the national landscape despite the efforts of men, especially those lording over big business, to keep the lid on. Rather than the cheerful housewife of advertising fiction, Friedan pulled the curtain to reveal "the purposeless, uncreative, even sexually joyless lives" of the suburban housewives who, because of the "feminine mystique...trap themselves in that one passion, one occupation, one role in life." According to Friedan, they were "doomed to suffer ultimately that bored, diffuse feeling of purposelessness, non-existence, non-involvement with the world that can be called *anomie*," and hence live desperate lives of "emptiness, idleness, boredom, alcoholism, drug addiction, disintegration to fat, disease, and despair after forty, when their sexual function has been filled."[2]

The blissful housewife, Friedan assures the reader, is merely a myth of the mystique, and she ought to know, for she was unable to find even one. "With a vision of the happy modern housewife as she is described by the magazines and television, by...sociologists,...educators, and the manipulators dancing before my eyes, I went in search of one of those mystical creatures. Like Diogenes [looking for a wise man] with his lamp, I went as a reporter from suburb to suburb, searching for a woman of ability and education who was fulfilled as a housewife."[3] Alas, all to no avail. She went to one "upper-income development," where she interviewed "twenty-eight wives" who appeared to exemplify the "mystique of feminine fulfillment."

> But what was mummy really like? Sixteen out of the twenty-eight were in analysis of analytical psychotherapy. Eighteen were taking tranquilizers; several had tried suicide; and some had been hospitalized for varying periods, for depression or vaguely diagnosed psychotic states. ("You'd be surprised at the number of these happy suburban wives who simply go berserk one night, and run shrieking through the street without any clothes on," said the local doctor, not a psychiatrist, who had been called in, in such emergencies.)...Twelve were engaged in extramarital affairs in fact or in fancy.[4]

And on and on it goes, page after morbid page, until the reader is depressed into submission to the baleful, cold reality of "the housewife's trap." "The problem that has no name," announces Friedan gravely, putting the final flourishes on *The Feminine Mystique*, "which is simply the fact that American women are kept from growing to their full human capacities...is taking a far greater toll on the physical and mental health of our country than any known disease."[5]

So it was that, through the ministrations of *The Feminine Mystique* housewifery became the cancer or AIDS of the 1960s. But how strong is her argument? Friedan's case that all or even most suburban housewives lead lives of unnamed desperation is shoddy. It is reasonable to suppose that some housewives other than Friedan fit her morose description, whether or not the cause was as she described. But some is quite different from all or most. As some doesn't make for a revolution, Friedan had to manipulate the reader's impressions accordingly. As a consequence, there is a lot of "I became aware of a growing body of evidence much of which has not been reported publicly because it does not fit current modes of thought about women,"[6] which is good sign that the author was trying to grow much of the evidence herself. There is a great deal of anecdotal evidence that would be difficult, if not impossible, to verify ("I sat in the office of another old-timer, one of the few women editors left in the women's magazine world..."[7]; "A therapist at another college told me of girls who..."[8]; "When I was interviewing on college campuses in the late fifties, chaplains and sociologists alike testified..."[9]; "Later, when I saw this same pattern repeated over and over again in similar suburbs, I knew it could hardly be a coincidence..."[10]; "While I never found a woman who actually fitted that 'happy housewife' image..."[11]). Or worse, the anecdotal evidence comes pre-upholstered with her conclusions ("Recently, interviewing high-school girls who had started out full of promise and talent, but suddenly stopped their education, I began to see new dimensions to the problem of feminine conformity."[12]) Or perhaps most offensive of all, the cobbling of anecdote into pseudo-law ("I noticed this pattern again and again, as I interviewed women..." is transformed into, for example, "The more a woman is deprived of function in society at the level of her own ability, the more her housework, mother-work, wife-work will expand—and the more she will resist finishing her housework or mother-work...."[13]). While anecdotal impressions have their place (one thinks of Tocqueville's masterful analysis in *Democracy in America*), they can all too easily be used as a substitutes for deeper analysis that might well contradict the surface sketch.

Sometimes the anecdotal is coupled with runaway rhetoric that takes the place of proof, such as her claim that a *McCall's* article titled "The Mother Who Ran Away" "brought the highest readership of any article they had ever run," resulting in the response of a former editor that "'We suddenly realized that all those women at home with their three and a half children were miserably unhappy.'"[14] This article was published in 1956. *McCall's* had been published (starting under a different name) for more than seventy-five years. Could the article really have had the highest readership ever? Measured by what? How? Even if there was a heady response to the article, and all the responses were positive, would that have meant that "*all* those women at home with their three-and-a-half children were miserably unhappy"?

Other times cumulative "evidence" is strung together into bizarre conclusions, the strangeness of which was apparently lost on Friedan. She cites a study of Green, Massachusetts, where loveless parents (mostly Polish immigrants) routinely brutalized their rebellious children. Friedan reports that the regularly beaten and neglected children suffered no psychological damage because "their mothers, like their fathers, worked all day in the factories." According to Friedan, the researcher conducting the study wondered whether "the very absence of this omnipresent nurturing mother love might explain why these children did not suffer the neurotic symptoms so commonly found in the sons of middle-class parents."[15] So it's much better to be unloved, neglected, and beaten than smothered by motherly love?

It would seem so—even when the data indicates otherwise. Though she concedes that many studies purport to show the detrimental effects on children whose mothers work, Friedan reads them differently, saying they "actually indicate that, where other conditions are equal, the children of mothers who work because they want to are less likely to be disturbed, have problems in school, or to 'lack a sense of personal worth' than housewives' children."[16] Further, she writes that there is "no definitive evidence that children are less happy, healthy, adjusted *because* their mothers work"[17] (though she cites only one article as proof). And indeed, the horrors of "maternal overprotection," she claims, are well documented in a "famous study" of "twenty mothers who had damaged their children to a pathological extent by 'material infantilization, indulgence and overprotection.'"[18]

Small wonder, then, that there was "increasing national awareness [by the mid-twentieth century] that something was wrong with American mothers." Is not the "real implication" of this swell of data "that the role of the middle-class American housewife forces many a mother to smother, absorb, the personality of both her sons and daughters?"[19]

Luckily there is a model for proper child-rearing—and it can be found behind the Iron Curtain:

> Not long ago Dr. Spock confessed, a bit uneasily, that Russian children, whose mothers usually have some purpose in their lives besides motherhood—they work in medicine, science, education, industry, government, art—seemed somehow more stable, adjusted, mature, than American children, whose full-time mothers do nothing but worry about them. Could it be that Russian

women are somehow better mothers because they have a serious purpose in their own lives?[20]

This hint of Marxism is telling. Despite her attempts to hide her
radical past, Friedan was not an innocent suburban housewife who
suddenly realized she was unrealized. She had been a Marxist
since her college days at Smith in the late 1930s and early 1940s.
In the years after, she belonged to, worked for, or wrote positively
about a string of leftist organizations and publications—like the
Popular Front, the Federated Press, *UE News*, Congress of American Women, *Jewish Life*—that had significant Communist membership or Soviet sympathies. Knowing that the call to revolution
in *The Feminine Mystique* would be damaged if it was associated with
the call to revolution in the *Communist Manifesto*, she hid her radical past. When Friedan biographer Daniel Horowitz brought it up
to her, the previously cooperative Friedan immediately closed the
lid on her private papers.[21]

But isn't this just redbaiting? Discrediting her later, mature work
on the basis of a youthful indiscretion? I think not. Friedan interpreted the fact that women were housewives in terms of a great
Marxian historical dialectic. In a chapter of *The Feminine Mystique*
devoted to critiquing fellow traveler Margaret Mead ("The Func-
tional Freeze, the Feminine Protest, and Margaret Mead"), she
argued that Mead failed to see that technology was overcoming
nature, and hence making obsolete sexual differences based upon
nature. In Samoa, where the modes of production are primitive
and, because of hot weather and scant clothing, the modes of
reproduction are evident, then defining a woman as wife and
mother makes sense because "having a baby" is the "pinnacle of
achievement." But Mead's Samoans lacked the "complex goals of
more advanced civilizations, in which instinct and environment are

increasingly controlled and transformed by the human mind."[22] In romanticizing the Samoans (a tendency Friedan ultimately blames on Mead's reliance on Freud), Mead was helping entrap American women in the feminine mystique:

> Margaret Mead's eloquent pages made a great many American women envy the serene femininity of a bare-breasted Samoan, and try to make themselves into languorous savages, breasts unfettered by civilization's brassieres, and brains undisturbed by pallid man-made knowledge of the goals of human progress.[23]

Mead offered a "vision of the mystique...where women, by merely being women and bearing children, will earn the same respect accorded men for their creative achievements." The ill effect of this vision is that "femininity becomes more than its definition by society; it becomes a value which society must protect from the destructive onrush of civilization like the vanishing buffalo."[24] That makes Mead a dangerous reactionary, whose "words acquire the aura of a righteous crusade—a crusade against change."[25] Against the romance of primitivism, which grounds the feminine mystique in nature, progress means conquering the natural conditions that keep women from being defined by their sex.

As with Marxism, the creative-destructive onrush of technical progress will ultimately free human nature from the shackles of nature and obsolete culture. We can now see her focus on the upper-middle class suburban housewife in a new light. The suburban housewife was at the edge of the final stage of the great historical dialectic. She, not her husband, was the first creature freed by labor-saving devices, in the final overcoming of material conditions that defined human beings by their labor. The problem was that she was spending her leisure in house-bound boredom rather than in creative and socially constructive work outside the home.

But not Betty Friedan. Despite her attempt to portray herself as just one more innocent housewife trapped by the false consciousness of suburbia, Friedan was continually active in agitation, and save for a few months, was always focused on building her writing career, using her (and her husband Carl's) earnings to pay for the child care and maid service that freed her to do "creative" and "meaningful" work. Here again we see how much Friedan resembled her own mother: a fundamental distaste for domesticity and a passionate desire to make good as a writer. The difference was that in Friedan's case, she was not going to let her husband stand in the way. The result was a sad duplication of the bitterness of her childhood household, except that both Betty and Carl were given to dishing out physical as well as verbal abuse.

The bitterness was mollified by the feeling that she was in the advance guard of the revolution, the first to be released from the false consciousness of the feminine mystique. Privileged enough to be educated by radical college professors at the elite Smith College, and to live in an eleven-room house with three bathrooms and marble fireplaces in Rockland County, New York, while writing *The Feminine Mystique*, she had the intellectual preparation and leisure to act as the vanguard who would awaken other upper-middle-class white women.

Awaken them to do what? If we might crib from Marx and Engels's *German Ideology*, after the revolution, in Friedan's hoped-for society, government will provide day care for children and subsidize women's continuing education. Women could then hunt for bargains in the morning, fish for writing jobs in the afternoon, rear children in the evening, criticize art and literature after dinner, and never become solely a bargain-hunter, a writer-for-hire, a mother, or a critic.

As others have noted, Friedan's book was aimed at a revolution of a very small, elite group of upper-middle-class, intellectually inclined women who could be doctors, lawyers, writers, artists, physicists, architects, or actresses—the sort of people she lived with in Rockland County. She seemed unconcerned, in her own life and in the *Mystique*'s "New Life Plan for Women," with the emancipation of the women who cleaned the houses of the revolutionaries or took care of their children.

Well, then, what evils can we chalk up to Betty Friedan's *Feminine Mystique*? First, Friedan sowed discontent by demonizing the role of housewives and romanticizing working outside the home. As even her sympathetic biographer Daniel Horowitz notes, Friedan presented a distorted view of the real situation and feelings of suburban housewives in the 1950s, reporting anything that was negative and suppressing anything that was positive, kneading the data to fit her need for a crisis and ignoring (as Marx did) anything that contradicted her grand, abstract thesis.[26]

Second, Friedan dragged Marx and Engels off the shop room floor and snuck them into the home. Examine this summary statement by Friedan of women's need to break free of the "housewife trap":

> [To] emancipate woman and make her the equal of the man is and remains an impossibility so long as the woman is shut out from socially productive labor and restricted to private domestic labor. The emancipation of woman will only be possible when woman can take part in production on a large, social scale, and domestic work no longer claims anything but an insignificant amount of her time.[27]

There are a number of statements like this throughout the *Mystique*. They reflect Friedan's passionate concern that suburban women not use their freedom merely to become community volunteers, but to get out into the professional workforce, where meaningful work really takes place.

The only difficulty is that this quote actually comes from chapter nine of Friedrich Engels's essay "The Origin of the Family, Private Property and the State." Friedan had copied it down during her research for the *Mystique*, and it entered into the stream of her own thinking. So no one can doubt that Engels expressed Friedan's thesis—or rather, that Friedan elaborated Engel's thesis.

Third, and most dishonorable of all, Friedan initially hid not only the radical roots but also the radical implications of her argument—although she fully intended these results. Nowhere, for instance, in the *Feminine Mystique* of 1963 do we find the word "abortion." Yet in later editions, we find in her added "Epilogue" (written in 1973, the same year as *Roe v. Wade*) a happy celebration of the necessity of abortion for her revolution:

> Society had to be restructured so that women, who happen to be the people who give birth, could make a human, responsible choice whether or not—and when—to have children, and not be barred thereby from participating in society in their own right. This meant the right to birth control and safe abortion; the right to maternity leave and child-care centers if women did not want to retreat completely from adult society during the childbearing years; and the equivalent of a GI bill for retraining if women chose to stay home with the children. For it seemed to me that most women would still choose to have children, though not so many if child rearing was no longer their only road to status and economic support—a vicarious participation in life.[28]

With Bernard Nathanson, Friedan started NARAL in 1969; the acronym then stood for the National Association for the Repeal of Abortion Laws. *Roe v. Wade* was their big victory. The right of a woman to kill her unborn child was necessary for her emancipation from being defined as a "mother." As with Marx, the passionate abstractness of the revolution leaves little time for concern over concrete and massive carnage. On rough calculation, the number of abortions in America since *Roe v. Wade* has been around 48,000,000, surpassing the number slaughtered by Lenin and Stalin in the name of communism.[29]

But that is not all. To ensure that "Occupation: Housewife" would become a distant memory, Friedan was a co-founder of NOW (the National Organization for Women). For Friedan, NOW was her dream agitating organization, allowing her the kind of prestige and acclaim she had long desired and the political clout necessary to effect the societal changes so that women would not be (in Engels's words) "shut out from socially productive labor and restricted to private domestic labor."

It is fair to say, as a kind of postscript, that Friedan long resisted the more radical elements of NOW (although not those of NARAL). She was not a "man-hater" (her phrase), nor was she sympathetic to lesbianism. On a charitable reading of her life and *The Feminine Mystique*, Friedan wanted both a happy home and at the same time freedom from its constraints to pursue what she considered to be more valuable and meaningful activities. Perhaps this is her most dangerous legacy. She helped spawn the notion that a combination of a very part time motherhood and full-time professional life was an achievable and desirable goal. Against almost all psychological research, she argued that children would feel loved if mothers gave them a kiss in the morning and a kiss at night, and left them to schools, day cares, and televisions in between.

Even on the left, there is a simmering rebellion against Friedan's vision, because it is recognized as a lie. Michelle Obama, wife of Democratic presidential candidate Barack Obama, confessed at a fund-raiser: "I don't know about you, but as a mother, wife, professional [with a $300,000 income], campaign wife, whatever it is that's on my plate, I'm drowning. And nobody's talking about these issues. In my adult lifetime, I felt duped." She continued, "People told me, 'You can do it all. Just stay the course, get your education, and you can raise a child, stay thin, be in shape, love your man, look good, and raise healthy children.' That was a lie." But then the only answer she can give is Friedan's: "America, Obama says, needs universal health care, access to child care, and better schools. And she, herself, is looking 'for someone—not just a woman—but someone who understands my struggles.'"[30] So goes the revolution.

A Conclusive Outline of Sanity

IN CASTING OUR EYES BACK ACROSS THE SMOKING RUBBLE OF THE twentieth century, we see a strange sight: humanity devouring itself for the sake of humanity. Russian religious philosopher Semyon Frank's words, brought forth again by Michael Burleigh, capture the painful paradox perhaps more clearly than any:

> Sacrificing himself for the sake of an idea, he does not hesitate to sacrifice other people for it. Among his contemporaries he sees either merely the victims of the world's evil he dreams of eradicating or the perpetrators of that evil.... This feeling of hatred for the enemies of the people forms the concrete and active psychological foundation of his life. Thus the great love of mankind of the future gives birth to a great hatred for people; the passion for organizing an earthly paradise becomes a passion for destruction.[1]

The hatred was all the more intense as it was directed at a real object: the people who stood in the way of trying to realize an unrealizable goal. The object of love, the utopian goal, continually receded just beyond the obstacles that called for destruction, thereby fueling both the passions of hate and love.

No one knows what the twenty-first century will hold. Much will depend on what we learn from the twentieth. The sweep of our fifteen books began in the Renaissance and ended with a crash half a millennium later. Can we gather, from what screwed up the world, what we might do to save it?

To ask such a question is to have slept through the lesson. In no small part, the carnage and confusion was caused by notions that the world, rather than human beings, needed to be saved from and for something. To save the world from political impotence, Machiavelli would have us embrace effective brutality. To save the world from skepticism, Descartes would have us become both more skeptical and more prideful. To save the world from industrial oppression, Marx and Lenin would have us annihilate half the world in revolution. To save the world from disease, poverty, and every social ill, Margaret Sanger and Adolf Hitler would have us eliminate the hordes of "unfit." To save the world from male oppression, Betty Friedan would have women kill their offspring.

Until the twentieth century, the notion of salvation had a decent pedigree. Now that the notion has been so tainted by its secular adherents, it will be a wonder if the idea of salvation itself can be saved. What all our authors have grasped, in one way or another, is that something is wrong and it needs to be righted. But they have also suffered acutely from one terrible insight: If God really does not exist, then it is all up to us. If this world is our only world, this life our only life, then it would seem that every effort, any means, and all passions fair or foul should be unleashed in an effort to transform the miseries of human life into a durable earthly happiness. If we all bang on the gates of paradise with our collective force, they must break open and allow humanity to enter, even though some will be lost in the crush.

If such is the result of rejecting the notion that it is man, and not primarily the world, that is fallen, then the way might be open to a very sober reassessment of an ancient insight. There's something profoundly wrong with *us*, some crack or deep taint that is largely incurable because it is largely invisible, a terrible twist that begins in the soul and curls its way outward. These are the threads of the screws that have screwed up the world.

The cracks in the soul become more visible when they are ignored. They become most visible when the twisted soul tries to rid the world of the very idea that each individual has a soul accountable to God. The twisted soul does this in order to deny its own twistedness, and that good and evil are defined by a divine source outside the self. The authors we've examined who have taken a turn at twisting the screws that have screwed up the world all have this in common. They all deny sin.

The ideas of God and sin might all seem too mythical for this scientific age until we recall that whether the bad thinker is Hobbes, Rousseau, Marx, or Freud, the authors we've covered in this book were mythmakers. They were enthralled by entirely mythical states of nature, entirely fictional alternative Edens, entranced by entirely impossible utopian paradises. Tens of millions of lives were offered up to the twin fictions of an alternative Garden of Eden and an alternative paradise, each taken and presented (falsely) as scientific fact.

In the heady eighteenth century, before atheism got its chance at the historical helm, it was possible to blame Christianity for every evil the Christian West had ever known. But after the twentieth century, when much of the world lay convulsed and broken upon the rock-hard certainties of so many secular political utopian schemes, atheism no longer has the luxury of speculating upon how grand the future will be once we've rid the world of priests and kings and brought heaven to earth. The old "myths" now seem to have a curious ring of truth. The safest place to put heaven, as some wise deity must have realized, is not on earth. As for our beginnings, we have found that if we create ourselves in the image of the savage, we end up with previously unimagined savagery.

We should dwell on this last point. We are so fond of thinking of our progress from the simple savage that we forget to take account of whether we are really progressing in some sort of virtue or rather becoming more complexly and deviously savage. We have a higher regard for health than our ancestors did, and a far greater knowledge of biology. But when biology, rather than theology, becomes the queen of the sciences, then Christian prohibitions against eugenics, the elimination of the unfit or the unwanted through abortion or infanticide, or the elimination of diseased races or classes all become merely "medieval" and irrelevant. Christian opposition to Kinsey's amoral analysis of bestiality, homosexuality, and pedophilia becomes ignorant and reactionary or even a "thought crime." By following the trajectory of these books that screwed up the world, we can wonder whether the advance of "science" over theology is an unmitigated good, and whether it is really progress. Perhaps it is bringing us to a new age of technological barbarism, wherein humanity becomes ever more religiously obsessed with health and sexual pleasure as pseudo-gods, sacrificing anything and everything to these twin deities.

What we can certainly say is that the intensity of humanity's self-destruction is a measure of the myth by which it lives, and this destruction is by no means limited to war and state-sponsored extermination. Kinsey bequeathed to us the intensity of sexual self-destruction, sexuality unleashed and directed to anything but fatherhood and motherhood. This destruction was foreshadowed in Hobbes's and Rousseau's respective states of nature, where raw and predatory sex, open and unleashed from any moral order, replaced an older notion of sexuality, secretive and bound up between a man and a woman and finding its natural outlet in the monogamous family, a family sanctified by God in the model of the Holy Family. The effect of Kinsey's liberation was the creation of a sexual state of nature, wherein fatherhood and motherhood fast disappear and thousands of children are daily sacrificed to the devouring Moloch of "abortion rights."

If the books we've covered offer an image of insanity, then perhaps by reversing the image and holding it up to a different light we can recover some outline of sanity. Perhaps we are not merely animals as Darwin would have it, but something more than animals. Perhaps we are not ghosts in machines, as Descartes would have it, but some other strange and glorious creature, something godlike but with two feet on the ground. Yet, being something godlike, we are not, as Nietzsche would have it, gods ourselves, but something far less, a faint but glowing resemblance to Someone else infinitely more resplendent. Perhaps there are dark corridors of our hearts that must be uncovered and exposed to light, as Freud would have it, but the darkness is not as hopelessly dark, and the light comes from another heart illumined by puncture and resurrection. Perhaps we do need a final revolution, as Marx and Lenin would have it, but it is a revolution from within and from above. Perhaps we should, as Mill bid us, seek the greatest happiness of the greatest number, but by filling our souls with unearthly joy rather than merely feeding our earthly pleasures like pigs. Perhaps, as Nietzsche howled, God did indeed die, but rose again, an *übermensch* of a very different kind, one that can save us from the madness of our own making.

Acknowledgments

I CONFESS—AND HAPPILY SO—THAT THE IDEA FOR THIS BOOK CAME from two sources. The first was my long experience teaching in Great Books programs at several different colleges and universities. The adjective "great," of course, is not a synonym for "good," but captures instead the simple and sorrowful truth that there are profoundly evil books as well as profoundly good ones. The second, more proximate, source was a feature in the national newsweekly *Human Events* called "The Ten Most Harmful Books of the Nineteenth and Twentieth Centuries."

I would also like to acknowledge the good humor and fine editorial guidance of Harry Crocker III, and the kind support of Bruce Schooley, Sam Reeves, and the To The Source Foundation. As ever, I am indebted to the love and support of my dear wife,

Teresa, and our children, all of whom sat patiently by as I crouched over the computer for so many months.

 **Notes**

CHAPTER ONE: *The Prince*

1. All quotations from Harvey Mansfield's translation of *The Prince* (Chicago: University of Chicago Press, 1985). As the chapters are so short, I have simply given the chapter numbers of all quotations in the text.

CHAPTER TWO: *Discourse on Method*

1. All quotations are taken from Donald Cress's translation of Descartes' *Discourse on Method* contained in René Descartes, *Discourse on Method and Meditations on First Philosophy* (Indianapolis, IN: Hackett Publishing, 1980). Copyright © 1998 by Hackett Publishing Company Inc. All rights reserved.
2. Alexis de Tocqueville, *Democracy in America*, translated by Henry Reeve, revised by Francis Bowen, further revisions by Phillips Bradley (New York: Random House), Vol. II, Chapter I, 3.

CHAPTER THREE: *Leviathan*

1. All quotations are taken from Thomas Hobbes, *Leviathan: or the Matter, Forme and Power of a Commonwealth Ecclesiasticall and Civil*, edited by Michael Oakeshott (New York: Collier, 1962). This quote comes from Book I, Chapter 6.
2. Book I, Chapter 13.
3. Ibid.
4. Ibid.
5. Book I, Chapter 14.
6. Ibid.
7. Ibid.

CHAPTER FOUR: *Discourse on the Origin and Foundations of Inequality among Men*

1. Jean-Jacques Rousseau, *Discourse on the Sciences and Arts* in Roger Masters, translator and editor, *The First and Second Discourses* (New York: St. Martin's Press, 1964), 36.
2. Ibid., 37.
3. Jean-Jacques Rousseau, *Discourse on the Origin and Foundations of Inequality among Men* in Masters, 102.
4. Ibid., 103.
5. Ibid., 120–121.
6. Ibid., 121.
7. Ibid., 135.
8. Ibid., 137.
9. Ibid., 142.
10. Ibid., 134–35.
11. Ibid., 134.
12. Ibid., 128.
13. Ibid., 129–30.

14. Ibid., 140.

15. Karl Marx and Friedrich Engels, *Manifesto of the Communist Party* in Lewis Feuer, editor, *Marx & Engels: Basic Writings on Politics and Philosophy* (Garden City, NY: Doubleday & Company, Inc., 1959), 41.

16. Rousseau, *Discourse on the Origin and Foundations of Inequality among Men*, in Masters, 117.

17. Ibid., 146.

18. Ibid., 141–42.

19. Ibid., 159.

20. Ibid., 160.

21. From Rousseau's *Confessions*, quoted in Leo Damrosch, *Jean-Jacques Rousseau: Restless Genius* (New York: Houghton Mifflin, 2005), 191–92.

CHAPTER FIVE: *The Manifesto of the Communist Party*

1. Francis Wheen, *Karl Marx: a Life* (New York: W. W. Norton & Company, 1999), 2–3.

2. Karl Marx and Friedrich Engels, *Manifesto of the Communist Party* in *Basic Writings on Politics and Philosophy*, edited by Lewis S. Feuer (Garden City, NY: Doubleday & Company, Inc., 1959), 6.

3. Quoted in Wheen, 135.

4. Marx and Engels, 7.

5. Ibid., 26–29.

6. See Plato's *Republic* and *Laws* and Aristotle's *Politics*, translations by Allan Bloom (New York: Basic Books, 2001), Thomas Pangle (Chicago: University of Chicago Press, 1988), and Carnes Lord (Chicago: University of Chicago Press, 1985), respectively.

7. Marx and Engels, 25–26.

CHAPTER SIX: *Utilitarianism*

1. From Max Lerner's introduction to John Stuart Mill, *Utilitarianism*, in *Essential Works of John Stuart Mill* (New York: Bantam Books, 1961), 185.

2. John Stuart Mill, *Autobiography*, in Lerner, 32.

3. Ibid., in Lerner, 13.

4. From Lerner's introduction to Mill, *Autobiography*, 3–4.

5. This assessment of Bentham by Mill occurred in the *London and Westminster Review* (August 1838) and is contained in John Stuart Mill, *Utilitarianism, On Liberty, Essay on Bentham*, Mary Warnock, ed. (New York: Meridian, 1962), 95–96.

6. Mill, *Autobiography*, in Lerner, 83.

7. Mill, *Utilitarianism*, in Lerner, 194.

8. For a more detailed examination of Epicurus's doctrines and the ill effect of their revival in modernity, readers may consult my *Moral Darwinism: How We Became Hedonists* (Downers Grove, IL: InterVarsity Press, 2002).

9. Mill, *Utilitarianism*, in Lerner, 199.

10. Ibid., 198. Emphasis added. Even more ludicrous, the judge will have to develop the fine discrimination necessary for comparing the incomparable and measuring the incommensurable. Imagine weighing on the same scale of utility (a) the pleasure of reading *Pride and Prejudice* while taking a long bath (b) the pleasure of eating a rare cheese washed down with an even rarer wine (c) the pleasure of being hugged by your seven-year-old daughter (d) the pleasure of hunting (e) the pleasure of watching Groucho Marx vex Margaret Dumont (f) the pleasure of hitting a baseball (g) the pleasure of a good nap. What common measure do they have? If the first rates a 4.2 and the fourth a 3.9 on the pleasure scale, the obvious question is 4.2 of what?

11. Ibid., 202.

CHAPTER SEVEN: *The Descent of Man*

1. Charles Darwin, *Origin of Species* (New York: Mentor, 1958), 29.
2. See my *Moral Darwinism: How We Became Hedonists* (Downers Grove, IL: InterVarsity Press, 2002).
3. Charles Darwin, *The Descent of Man, and Selection in Relation to Sex*, with an introduction by John Tyler Bonner and Robert M. May (Princeton, NJ: Princeton University Press, 1981), Part I, Chapter Five, 168.
4. Ibid., Part I, Chapter Five, 177.
5. George William Hunter, *A Civic Biology, Presented in Problems* (New York: American Book Company, 1914), 261.
6. Ibid., 262–63.
7. Ibid., 263.
8. Darwin, *The Descent of Man*, Part I, Chapter Five, 168.
9. Ibid., Part I, Chapter Three, 82.
10. Ibid., Part I, Chapter Five, 168–69.
11. Those still tempted to believe that eugenics was merely something cooked up by Hitler and a few simians from the SS should read Richard Weikart's *From Darwin to Hitler: Evolutionary Ethics, Eugenics, and Racism in Germany* (New York: Palgrave Macmillan, 2004); Edwin Black, *War against the Weak: Eugenics and America's Campaign to Create a Master Race* (New York: Four Walls Eight Windows, 2003); and Stefan Kühl, *The Nazi Connection: Eugenics, American Racism, and German National Socialism* (Oxford: Oxford University Press, 1994). .
12. Darwin, *The Descent of Man*, Part I, Chapter Three, 103.
13. Ibid., Part I, Chapter Seven, 235.
14. Ibid., Part I, Chapter Seven, 238.
15. Ibid., Part I, Chapter Six, 201.

CHAPTER EIGHT: *Beyond Good and Evil*

1. Friedrich Nietzsche, *The Gay Science*, Walter Kaufmann, trans. (New York: Vintage, 1974), section 125.
2. Charles Darwin, *The Descent of Man*, Part I, Chapter Five, 177.
3. Ibid., Part II, Chapter Twenty-One, 403.
4. Ibid., Part II, Chapter Twenty-One, 405.
5. Friedrich Nietzsche, *Beyond Good and Evil*, Walter Kaufmann, trans. (New York: Vintage, 1966), section 225.
6. Ibid., section 228.
7. Ibid., section 257.
8. Ibid., section 257.
9. Darwin, Part I, Chapter Five, 162–63.
10. Nietzsche, *Beyond Good and Evil*, section 258.
11. Ibid., section 259.
12. Ibid., section 4.
13. Ibid., section 13.
14. Ibid., section 259.
15. Ibid., section 260.
16. Ibid.
17. Ibid.
18. Ibid., section 62.
19. Ibid.
20. Ibid., section 195.
21. Ibid., section 44.
22. Ibid., section 203.
23. Ibid., section 251.
24. Ibid., section 208.
25. Ibid., sections 250–251.
26. See Curtis Cate, *Friedrich Nietzsche* (New York: Overlook Press, 2002), 546–47.
27. Ibid., 559.

CHAPTER NINE: *The State and Revolution*

1. V. I. Lenin, *The State and Revolution*, in Lenin, *Essential Works of Lenin* (New York: Dover, 1987), Chapter I, Section 1, 272

2. Ibid., Chapter I, Section 1, 274.

3. Ibid., Chapter V, Section 4, 347.

4. Ibid., Chapter I, Section 4, 282.

5. Ibid., Chapter I, Section 4, 280–81.

6. Ibid., Chapter V, Section 4, 343.

7. These are the words, and conservative estimates, of Zbigniew Brzezinski, *Out of Control* (New York: Simon & Schuster, 1993), 11.

8. By this we mean not just acting according to Machiavelli's counsels in a general way, but being directly influenced by reading Machiavelli. See Robert Service, *Lenin: A Biography* (Cambridge, MA: Belknap Press, 2000), 8–10, 203–04, 376.

9. Dmitri Volkogonov, *Autopsy for an Empire: The Seven Leaders Who Built the Soviet Regime* (New York: The Free Press, 1998), 80.

10. Lenin, Chapter I, Section 1, 273.

11. Ibid.

12. Ibid., Chapter I, Section 1, 274.

13. Ibid., Chapter II, Section 1, 288.

14. Ibid.

15. Quoted in Service, 395.

16. Ibid., Chapter III, Section 3, 307.

17. Ibid., Chapter V, Section 2, 337.

18. Service, 87.

19. Lenin, Chapter II, Section 1, 288.

20. Ibid., Chapter V, Section 2, 339.

CHAPTER TEN: *The Pivot of Civilization*

1. See Edwin Black, *War against the Weak: Eugenics and America's Campaign to Create a Master Race* (New York: Four Walls Eight

Windows, 2003), and Stefan Kühl, *The Nazi Connection: Eugenics, American Racism, and German National Socialism* (Oxford: Oxford University Press, 1994).

2. Margaret Sanger, *The Pivot of Civilization* (Lenox, MA: Hard Press, 2006), Chapter One, 17.

3. Ibid., Chapter Eight, 74.

4. Ibid., 75.

5. Ibid., Chapter Four, 37.

6. Charles Darwin, *The Descent of Man*, Part I, Chapter Three, 92.

7. Ibid., 102. Emphasis added.

8. Ibid., Part I, Chapter Five, 174.

9. Ibid., Part I, Chapter Four, 122.

10. Ibid., 146.

11. Sanger, Chapter Four, 41.

12. Ibid., 43.

13. Ibid.

14. Ibid., 44.

15. Ibid., Chapter Five, 48; 75,000 out of a population of 783,000.

16. Ibid., Chapter Three, 27.

17. Ibid., Chapter Twelve, 102.

18. Ibid., Chapter Five, 49.

19. Ibid., Chapter Eight, 71.

20. Ibid., Chapter Five, 49–50.

21. Ibid., Chapter Six, 56.

22. Ibid., 58.

23. Ibid.

24. Ibid., Chapter Nine, 85.

25. Ibid., Chapter Ten, 89.

26. Ibid., 91.

27. Ibid., Chapter Ten, 91.

28. Ibid., Chapter Ten, 91–92.

29. Ibid., 91.

30. Ibid., Chapter Twelve, 103.

31. Ibid., 104.

32. Ibid., 106.

33. Ibid., Chapter Eight, 69.

CHAPTER ELEVEN: *Mein Kampf*

1. Both quoted in Alan Bullock, *Hitler and Stalin: Parallel Lives* (New York: Vintage, 1993), 803.

2. On this episode see John Toland, *Adolf Hitler* (New York: Doubleday, 1976), 676–77.

3. Hugh Gallagher, *By Trust Betrayed: Patients, Physicians, and the License to Kill in the Third Reich*, revised edition (Arlington, VA: Vandamere, 1995), 9, 86.

4. Quoted in Robert Lifton, *The Nazi Doctors* (New York: Basic Books, 2000), 31.

5. Ibid., 32.

6. Ibid., 30.

7. Ibid.

8. Adolf Hitler, *Mein Kampf* (Mumbai: Jaico Publishing House, 1988), Volume I, Chapter Eight, 195. The preferred translation of *Mein Kampf* would be the so-called "Reynal & Hitchcock" (R & H) edition of 1939, made under the auspices of Alvin Johnson and published by Houghton Mifflin. Unfortunately, it is out of print, so I have used the Jaico edition. The R & H has the more accurate "program-maker" instead of the Jaico's "political philosopher" in Volume I, Chapter Eight, 283–87. But the distinction that Hitler makes is in important respects the same one Plato makes. Of course, Plato was infinitely more subtle, and undertakes to illuminate the true good, not the fanciful evil.

9. Hitler, *Mein Kampf,* Volume I, Chapter Eight, 194.

10. Ibid., Volume I, Chapter Eight, 195. Interested readers should consult the R & H translation, Chapter Eight, 283–85.

11. Ibid.

12. Ibid., 196–97.

13. Ibid., 196.

14. Michael Burleigh, *Sacred Causes: The Clash of Religion and Politics, from the Great War to the War on Terror* (New York: Harper-Collins, 2007), 94–95, 99–122.

15. Hitler, Volume I, Chapter One, 26.

16. Ibid., Volume I, Chapter Two, 32.

17. Ibid., 38.

18. Ibid., 39.

19. Ibid.

20. Ibid., Volume I, Chapter Eleven, 285.

21. Ibid., Volume I, Chapter Three, 97.

22. Ibid., Volume I, Chapter Two, 40–42.

23. Ibid., 48, 58, 62, 66.

24. Ibid., Volume I, Chapter Eleven, 299.

25. Ibid., 297.

26. Ibid., Volume I, Chapter Four, 146.

27. Ibid.

28. Ibid., 149.

29. Ibid.

30. Ibid.

31. Ibid., Volume I, Chapter Five, 164.

32. Ibid., Volume I, Chapter Ten, 241–42.

33. Ibid., Volume II, Chapter One, 346.

34. Ibid., 223–24.

35. Ibid., Volume I, Chapter Five, 164.

36. Ibid., Volume I, Chapter Ten, 242.

37. Friedrich Nietzsche, *Beyond Good and Evil,* section 61.

38. Hitler, Volume II, Chapter One, 339.

39. Ibid., 346.

40. Ibid., 348–49.

CHAPTER TWELVE: *The Future of an Illusion*

1. Peter Gay, Freud: *A Life for Our Time* (New York: W. W. Norton, 1998), 526.

2. Quoted in ibid., 527.

3. Sigmund Freud, *The Future of an Illusion,* James Strachey, trans. (New York: W. W. Norton, 1961), Chapters One–Two, 6–12.

4. Ibid., Chapter Two, 13.

5. Ibid., Chapter Three, 18.

6. Ibid., Chapter Seven, 45 and also 47.

7. Ibid., Chapter Two, 13.

8. Jean-Jacques Rousseau, *The Social Contract*, Roger Masters, ed., Judith Masters, trans. (New York: St. Martin's Press, 1978), Book I, Chapter One, 46.

9. Freud, *The Future of an Illusion*, Chapter Four, 29.

10. Ibid.

11. Ibid., 27.

12. Ibid., 30.

13. Gay, 332–33.

14. Ibid., 334.

15. From Freud, *Moses and Monotheism*, Chapter Twenty-Three, 131, as quoted in Gay, 334, footnote. Emphasis added.

16. Freud, *The Future of an Illusion*, Chapter Six, 39–40.

17. Ibid., 40.

18. Ibid., 42.

19. Ibid., 41–42.

20. Ibid., Chapter Eight, 54.

21. Ibid., 51–52.

22. Ibid., Chapter Nine, 63.

23. Ibid., Chapter Ten, 67.

CHAPTER THIRTEEN: *Coming of Age in Samoa*

1. Margaret Mead, *Coming of Age in Samoa: A Psychological Study of Primitive Youth for Western Culture* (American Museum of Natural History Special Members edition, 1928, 1973), Chapter One, 3.

2. Ibid., Chapter Two, 8.

3. Ibid., Chapter Fourteen, 137.

4. Ibid., Chapter Four, 24.

5. Ibid., Chapter Thirteen, 119.

6. Ibid., 118.

7. Ibid., 119.

8. Ibid., Chapter Seven, 58.

9. Ibid., 54.

10. Ibid., 50.

11. Ibid., Chapter Ten, 84.

12. Ibid., 87.

13. Ibid., 76.

14. Ibid., 82.

15. Ibid., 83.

16. Ibid., Chapter Seven, 60.

17. Ibid., Chapter Ten, 83.

18. Ibid., Chapter Thirteen, 124.

19. Ibid., 110.

20. Ibid., 112.

21. Ibid., Chapter Seven, 55.

22. Ibid., Chapter Nine, 70.

23. Ibid., Chapter Eleven, 91.

24. Ibid., Chapter Fourteen, 138.

25. Ibid., 138.

26. Derek Freeman, *Margaret Mead and Samoa: The Making and Unmaking of an Anthropological Myth* (Cambridge, MA: Harvard University Press, 1983), 109.

27. See Hilary Lapsley, *Margaret Mead and Ruth Benedict: The Kinship of Women* (Amherst, MA: University of Massachusetts Press, 1999), 26, 76, 79–80, 308.

28. Jane Howard, *Margaret Mead: A Life* (New York: Fawcett Crest, 1984), 253.

29. Martin Orans, *Not Even Wrong: Margaret Mead, Derek Freeman, and the Samoans* (Novato, CA: Chandler and Sharp Publishers, Inc., 1996), 123–24.

30. Ibid., 124.

31. Ibid., 125.

32. Ibid., 13.

CHAPTER FOURTEEN: *Sexual Behavior in the Human Male*

1. Alfred Kinsey, Wardell Pomeroy, Clyde Martin, *Sexual Behavior in the Human Male* (Philadelphia and London: W. B. Saunders Company, 1948), 7.

2. Ibid., Chapter Twenty-Two, 667. Emphases added.

3. Ibid., 668.

4. Ibid.

5. Ibid.

6. Ibid., 669.

7. Ibid., 671.

8. Ibid., 677.

9. Ibid.

10. Ibid., 678.

11. Ibid.

12. Jonathan Gathorne-Hardy, *Kinsey: Sex the Measure of All Things* (Bloomington, IN: Indiana University Press, 1998), 337.

13. Kinsey, Pomeroy, and Martin, Chapter Twenty-One, 617.

14. Ibid., 623.
15. Ibid., 639.
16. Judith Reisman and Edward Eichel, *Kinsey, Sex, and Fraud* (Lafayette, LA: Huntington House, 1990), 29, 52–53.
17. James Jones, *Alfred C. Kinsey: A Public/Private Life* (New York: Norton, 1997), 387
18. Kinsey, Pomeroy, and Martin, Chapter Twenty-One, 656.
19. Ibid., 659–60.
20. Ibid., Chapter Five, 176–77.
21. Ibid., 179.
22. Ibid., 178.
23. Ibid., 181.

CHAPTER FIFTEEN: *The Feminine Mystique*

1. Betty Friedan, *The Feminine Mystique* (new introduction and Epilogue by the author) (New York: Bantam Doubleday Dell, 1983), 15.
2. Ibid., 179, 181, 208.
3. Ibid., 233.
4. Ibid., 234–35.
5. Ibid., 364.
6. Ibid., 31.
7. Ibid., 56.
8. Ibid., 176.
9. Ibid., 188.
10. Ibid., 235.
11. Ibid., 236.
12. Ibid., 72–73.
13. Ibid., 238–39.
14. Ibid., 50.
15. Ibid., 199–200.

16. Ibid., 195–96.

17. Ibid., 194.

18. Ibid., 198.

19. Ibid., 202.

20. Ibid., 197.

21. See introduction, Daniel Horowitz, *Betty Friedan and the Making of* The Feminine Mystique*: The American Left, the Cold War, and Modern Feminism* (Amherst: University of Massachusetts Press, 1998).

22. Friedan, 140–41.

23. Ibid., 143.

24. Ibid., 142–43.

25. Ibid., 144.

26. Horowitz, 209–10.

27. Ibid., 201.

28. Friedan, 385–86.

29. From the Guttmacher Institute (http://www.guttmacher.org/pubs/fb_induced_abortion.html).

30. As reported on http://www.barackobama.com/2007/08/22/its_all_about_priorities_for_m.php.

AFTERWORD: A Conclusive Outline of Sanity

1. Michael Burleigh, *Sacred Causes* (New York: HarperCollins, 2007), 39.

Index

R

S